# TRANSFORMED LIVES

*Making Sense of Atonement Today*

## CYNTHIA S.W. CRYSDALE

Seabury Books
NEW YORK

Unless otherwise noted, the Scripture quotations contained herein are from the New Revised Standard Version Bible, copyright © 1989 by the Division of Christian Education of the National Council of Churches of Christ in the U.S.A. Used by permission. All rights reserved.

Cover design by Laurie Klein Westhafer, Bounce Design
Typeset by Denise Hoff

A catalog record of this book is available from the Library of Congress.

ISBN-13: 978-1-59627-268-2 (print)

ISBN-13: 978-1-59627-269-9 (ebook)

Seabury Books
19 East 34th Street
New York, New York 10016

www.churchpublishing.org

An imprint of Church Publishing Incorporated

*Printed in the United States of America*

*To John Govan, SJ*

*a faithful guide in/with/through*

*multiple deaths and resurrections*

# Contents

# Acknowledgments

As is the case with most projects, there are a host of people who have contributed to my work on this book. While it is not possible to name them all, a few individuals and institutions deserve special mention. First and foremost, I want to thank Karen Meridith, director of Education for Ministry, for suggesting this project in the first place, and Nancy Bryan of Church Publishing for endorsing the idea. Further, my work was enhanced immeasurably by a small reading group of colleagues and friends who read through each chapter with me, making suggestions large and small. Their willingness to work with me on this made the writing a pleasure rather than a chore. Elsa Bakkum, Karen Meridith, Mary Ann Patterson, Cathy Uffen, and Sissy Wile made up this group. Others read parts of the work and made helpful comments—these include Peter Laughlin, Rob MacSwain, and Neil Ormerod. I owe a special debt of gratitude to Chris Bryan and Paul Holloway who took the time to carefully review the material on the New Testament and provided extensive feedback. Finally, there are a number of colleagues whose own work contributed significantly to my thinking on atonement: Charles Hefling, Jennifer Jackson, Peter Laughlin, William Loewe, Giles Mongeau, and Gerard Sloyan.

Developing one's idea is always enriched through engagement with students on a topic. Two sets of students at two different institutions have thus indirectly aided this book. Rachel Bush-Erdman, Mollie Roberts, and Diana Scheide took "Reading Redemption" with me at the School of Theology of the University of the South, while John Andrade, Margarida Da Silva, Nicole De Francesco, and Gail Tymchuk took a similar course at St. Jerome's University. Thanks for their patience and willingness to think theologically with me. These two institutions likewise deserve mention. The School of Theology at the University of the South employs me full-time and encourages my scholarship. The university granted me a sabbatical during the 2013–2014 academic year and supported it with travel funds. I spent that sabbatical at St. Jerome's University at the University of Waterloo in Ontario, Canada. My thanks goes to St. Jerome's and their staff for adopting me as a visiting scholar: Cristina Vanin suggested my visiting professorship in the first place; John Rempel and David Seljak lent me their offices while they were away on their own sabbaticals; and Christian Schwendinger aided the bureaucratic processes. Finally, the Conant Fund of The Episcopal Church gave me financial support in aid of the sabbatical. None of this work would have been completed without this institutional support.

Special thanks go to my husband, Peter Hunter. The two years that it took to research and write this book coincided with the first two years of our marriage. While he likes to think of himself as a "kept man," he has done a lot of "keeping" of me during this time: housework, paying bills, entertaining me, and otherwise diverting me from fixation on productivity. His sense of humor and practical outlook on life kept me grounded in the real world while I thought lofty thoughts and pondered mysteries well beyond my ken.

# Introduction

## Problems with the Atonement

I have found over and over again that mature Christians, when confronted with the topic of "atonement," roll their eyes in despair and/or change the topic. Faithful Christians, even very engaged, educated, and intentional believers, are at a loss when asked to explain why Jesus died on the cross or what it means to say that Jesus died for our sins. Sunday schools continue to promote views that leave kids saying things like "Jesus I like, but the Father seems pretty mean!" Others want to know "Why is God always so angry?"[1]

In the last several decades, scholarly literature and media discussion around the Christian doctrine of "atonement" has multiplied. There are those who, for a variety of reasons, find the idea that God intended his son's violent death appalling. There are others who have found it necessary, hence, to review traditional interpretations of Jesus's death. They do this in order either to explain the appalling parts as not so appalling after all, or to put forth an account of salvation not so dependent on a violent sacrifice. At a commonsense level, believers are finding it hard to find relevance in a narrative of a sacrificial and necessary death on the part of God's son. The dilemmas of their lives don't find any "purchase" in a theological explanation of salvation that supposedly relieves them of guilt because Jesus has already "paid the price" for their sins.

So just what is atonement and why are there problems with it?

---

1 Mark D. Baker and Joel B. Green, *Recovering the Scandal of the Cross: Atonement in New Testament and Contemporary Contexts* (Downers Grove, IL: InterVarsity Press, 2011), 46.

Let's begin in the broadest possible way, by discussing what we call the *work* of Christ. This is in contrast to the *person* of Christ, which is an equally important topic. Theological explanations about the *person* of Christ have to do with *who* he was, while the *work* of Christ generates a set of questions about *what he did*; what difference did he make in the world or in our lives? Both sets of questions arose very shortly after Jesus's life ended. In fact, the earliest church was quick to jump on the "What difference does he make?" question, because they knew their lives had been changed. They had to make sense of their changed lives and explain how these were connected to Jesus's life, death, and resurrection. Determining, in light of this, just who Jesus was, relative to God the Father, came in due course. The two topics were then intimately related in theological debates as the church moved into its self-definition in the first four centuries.[2]

Within this broad question about the *work* of Christ—the difference that his coming into history made—we can address atonement in the broadest sense of the word. Atonement is an English word, without Greek or Latin roots, that means what it says—"at-one-ment." Atonement is about reconciliation of estranged parties. With regard to God, it is about bringing the created order back into relationship with its Creator. It presumes brokenness or alienation of some kind. So the short answer to what difference the Christ event made in history is that it brought us back into relationship with God. So Paul tells us, "In Christ God was reconciling the world to himself" (2 Cor. 5:19).

But if we delve a bit deeper, further questions arise: How did the events of Jesus's life, death, and resurrection bring this about? What is the means by which this reconciliation became possible? As we will see as the book unfolds, there are many ways these questions have been answered—multiple metaphors, images, and explanatory accounts of how this reconciliation has been brought about. But over the years atonement has gained a much narrower meaning, in reference to a certain way that reconciliation has been accomplished. It has its roots historically in St. Anselm and his work *Cur Deus Homo?* in the eleventh century. His basic model of "satisfaction"—of Christ satisfying God's justice on

---

2 On the early church and its theological debates, see Henry Chadwick, *The Early Church* (London: Penguin Books, 1993).

behalf of humans—came to dominate the tradition.[3] Yet it also came to be transposed into a view that highlighted a legal and punitive worldview at the same time it turned Christ's death into a violent act on God's part.

So we come to what Anthony Tambasco calls the "the popular view" of atonement.[4] This commonly held understanding of the means by which Christ reconciles the world to God has a number of components. It focuses primarily on the crucifixion, and it sees the crucifixion as a punishment. This is the punishment of death that all humans deserve, since all have "fallen short of the glory of God." While we deserve this death/punishment, Jesus suffered it instead of us on the cross so that his punishment yields our salvation. This was God's plan from the start. Thus we are saved without undergoing the punishment that we duly deserve for our sins.

What Tambasco calls the "popular view" has a more technical name. It has been titled the "penal substitutionary view of atonement." "Penal" indicates that the focus is on punishment, as in a court of law. "Substitutionary" has to do with the idea that Christ suffered death in place of what we should have suffered. The focus is on a kind of transaction whereby an exchange took place, instigated by God the Father and carried out by God the Son.[5]

It is precisely this penal substitutionary account of the means of reconciliation (the narrower meaning of atonement) that has run into problems of late. At the commonsense level, it has become a barrier for many in their faith lives. Its terms of reference seem too remote historically as well as off-putting at the symbolic and psychic levels: this is not a God who welcomes one into a healing relationship.

In theological discourse recent critics have pointed out that this account is both too narrow in its scope and an inaccurate account of the

---

3 Note that, while questions about *who* Christ was came to be the subject of church councils and therefore official doctrinal definition in the third and fourth centuries CE, Christ's *work* and how his entrance into history provided us with reconciliation has never been the subject of doctrinal definition.

4 Anthony J. Tambasco, *A Theology of Atonement and Paul's Vision of Christianity* (Collegeville, MN: Liturgical Press, 1991).

5 This view also is referred to as the "forensic" or "vicarious" model of the atonement. Robert D. Hughes refers to it as "the late evangelical theory of substitutionary, vicarious, penal atonement" and suggests that, though it is hard to pin down historically, it seems to have its nascence in late English puritanism. See Robert Davis Hughes, "What a Friend We Have in Jesus," *Sewanee Theological Review* 35 (1992): 247–63, esp. 250.

heart of the tradition. It does not, as it stands, carry the full weight of biblical warrant. It incorporates a view of sacrifice that does not accord with sacrifice as understood or practiced in the Jewish tradition. It involves reading the New Testament, particularly Paul, without properly contextualizing him and his missionary work in the world of the first century of the Common Era. Likewise, Anselm's notion of satisfaction is misunderstood in terms of modern European justice systems rather than in terms of the feudal world for which it was meant. The penal view reflects an individualistic, legalistic, and transactional mentality current in the modern world but not current in earlier sources of the tradition. As Mark Baker and Joel Green conclude: "In short, it is unclear whether the atonement model of penal satisfaction is sufficiently critical of the cultural influences of the modern era that, at the very least, contribute to the reductionism of the saving work of Christ along mechanistic and individualistic lines."[6]

In fact, there have been throughout Christianity, beginning with the New Testament record, a host of ways in which the work of Christ has been described. Robert Hughes refers to being "embarrassed by an abundance of riches" in a consideration of atonement writ large. He finds twenty-one "root metaphors" that he groups into three large categories: incarnational, messianic, and atonement-center (in the narrower focus on Jesus's death and resurrection).[7] In spite of these riches, the Christian faith continues to be perceived in the narrower caricature of a God who engineered a violent solution to the woes of mankind. An online search of "Jesus died for our sins" yields websites promoting the notion that Jesus saved us by dying in our place on the cross.[8] Richard Dawkins, a learned scientist and atheist says that "the atonement, the central doctrine of Christianity [is] vicious, sado-masochistic and repellent."[9] He

---

6 Baker and Green, *Recovering the Scandal,* 43.

7 See Hughes, "What a Friend," 250.

8 See, for example, http://www.cbn.com/spirituallife/churchandministry/evangelism/Butts_Why_ Jesus_Died.aspx; http://christianity.stackexchange.com/questions/8785/what-does-it-mean-to-say-jesus-died-for-our-sins; and http://www.gotquestions.org/Jesus-died-for-our-sins.html. The one exception is a discussion by Brian Zahnd that provides a more nuanced set of reflections. See http://brianzahnd.com/2014/04/dying-sins-work/. All websites accessed June 13, 2015.

9 Richard Dawkins, *The God Delusion* (Boston: Houghton Mifflin, 2006), 253, as quoted in Michael R. Stead, ed., *Christ Died for Our Sins: Essays on the Atonement* (Canberra, Australia: Barton Books, 2013), 1. The introduction to this set of essays, published by The Doctrine Commission of the General Synod of the Anglican Church of Australia, provides a concise review of the main themes in Christian atonement theology. See pp. 1–10.

believes the atonement is based on a theory in which God demands the death of his son to appease his anger at sin.

Dawkins is neither a theologian nor a Christian and portrays a caricature of the Christian gospel. Nevertheless, even at the more refined level of academic discourse, atonement theory has come under great scrutiny in recent years. This literature of critique is abundant and comes from three streams of thought. First, Christian feminists have used a "hermeneutic of suspicion" in analyzing ways in which the tradition has demonized women.[10] Within this general trend, a theology indicating that God solved the problem of sin via punishment of his incarnate Son promotes suffering and violence as positive forces of change. For centuries and across cultures, women have been admonished to imitate Christ in his suffering. This admonition then serves as a justification for abusive treatment of women. So feminists have pointed out that theological models are not benign, and that an atonement theology that hinges on suffering or punishment as the central cause of salvation promotes concrete abusive practices.[11] A similar story has been told with regard to non-Anglo-European cultures, whereby the cross has served as an instrument of justified torture of persons considered less than human and therefore more sinful and in greater need of "salvation."[12]

In addition to this critique of power and its abuse, a second broad swath of writings falls under the label of "non-violent atonement" theories. Some of these books and articles have been generated by scholars from explicitly pacifist denominations, such as J. Denny Weaver's *The Nonviolent Atonement.*[13] Others simply raise the question of how the heart of the gospel can incorporate violence as the solution to the problem of evil and sin. So writers have generated a discussion through books with titles such as *Stricken by God? Nonviolent Identification and the*

---

10 See Cynthia S. W. Crysdale, *Embracing Travail: Retrieving the Cross Today* (New York: Continuum, 1999), 72–76.

11 The most pointed of these critiques is JoAnn Carlson Brown and Carole Bohn, eds., *Christianity, Patriarchy and Abuse: A Feminist Critique* (New York: Pilgrim Press, 1989). For a review of this literature, see Flora A. Keshgegian, "The Scandal of the Cross: Revisiting Anselm and His Feminist Critics," *Anglican Theological Review* 82 (2000): 476–79, and Baker and Green, *Recovering the Scandal,* 47, esp. n43.

12 See, for example, Yacob Tesfai, *The Scandal of a Crucified World: Perspectives on the Cross and Suffering* (New York: Orbis Books, 1994). See also Crysdale, *Embracing Travail,* 104–8.

13 J. Denny Weaver, *The Nonviolent Atonement,* 2nd ed. (Michigan: Eerdmans, 2011).

*Victory of Christ*[14] or *Problems with Atonement*[15] followed by *Options on Atonement in Christian Thought.*[16] The center of this critique lies in the fact that penal substitutionary theories of atonement end up placing violence at the heart of God's character. If God actively intended (not merely permitted) the execution of Jesus on the cross, God in Godself becomes complicit in the violence that is otherwise the basis of sin. A corollary of this is that this view of salvation pits one person of the Trinity against another: God the Father needed to kill God the Son in order to bring salvation to humankind.

A final burgeoning of literature revolves around the work of René Girard. Girard (b. 1923) is a French-born cultural historian and philosopher who developed the notion of mimetic rivalry as the foundation of human culture. All human desires are mimetic, that is, based on imitation of those we admire. Conflict arises from mimetic rivalry; we become jealous of those whom we both admire and resent. Religion and its rituals save groups from acting out this rivalry, especially through the scapegoat mechanism whereby the group takes out its jealousy on one person and excludes that person from society. Interestingly, while one could easily interpret Jesus's death as such a mechanism for relieving group tensions through violence, Girard maintains that the biblical tradition acts to reverse such violence, particularly in the death and resurrection of Jesus. He sees the Christ event as providing a way out of this cycle of violence, since the attempt to use Jesus as a scapegoat (by power mongers in his day) failed miserably, with the victory of the risen Lord revealing such human power as ultimately impotent.[17] This analysis of violence and human desire, and its reversal, has provided much grist for the mill for creating new ways to understand the work of Christ in salvation history.[18]

---

14 Brad Jersak and Michael Hardin, *Stricken by God?: Nonviolent Identification and the Victory of Christ* (Grand Rapids, MI: Eerdmans, 2007).

15 Stephen Finlan, *Problems with Atonement* (Collegeville, MN: Liturgical Press, 2005).

16 Stephen Finlan, *Options on Atonement in Christian Thought* (Collegeville, MN: Liturgical Press, 2007).

17 René Girard, *I See Satan Fall Like Lightning*, trans. James G. Williams (Maryknoll, NY: Orbis Books, 2001). For more on Girard, see http://en.wikipedia.org/wiki/René_Girard. Accessed June 13, 2015.

18 See Raymund Schwager, *Jesus in the Drama of Salvation: Toward a Biblical Doctrine of Redemption*, trans. James G. Williams and Paul Haddon (New York: Crossroad, 1999) and *Banished from Eden: Original Sin and Evolutionary Theory in the Drama of Salvation*, trans. James G. Williams (London: Gracewing, 2005). See also Gil Bailie, *Violence Unveiled: Humanity at the Crossroads* (New York: Crossroad, 1995) and S. Mark Heim, *Saved from Sacrifice: A Theology of the Cross* (Grand Rapids, MI: Eerdmans, 2006).

This book takes these criticisms for granted. Rather than rehearse the problems, my goal is to review and retrieve the best of the tradition, with the conviction that violence does not lie at the heart of what was accomplished by the entrance of the second person of the Trinity into history. Within this general goal there are multiple tasks. One is to describe and give examples of what in fact goes on in people's lives today when they find themselves changed by an encounter with God (chapter one). Secondly, I delve into the biblical traditions generated by Jesus and Paul to grasp the meanings they convey about God's entrance into history in the events of Jesus's life, death, and resurrection (chapter two). I add to this a sampling of ways in which theologians in the first millennium of the church's history expanded on these meanings, as well as illustrations of the piety that devotion to the cross generated in the Middle Ages (chapter three). Thirdly, it is essential to grasp the ways in which our cultural world is distinctive, after the rise of modern science, the introduction of industrial-technological innovations, and the emergence of modern democracies. Hence, I trace developments in cultural expectations as science moved into the modern era and the "discovery of discovery" yielded an emphasis on individual autonomy and human agency (chapter four). This has led to a drastic shift in assumptions not only about the normativity of Anglo-European culture but about the entire enterprise of theology (chapter five). Finally, I present a current interpretation of atonement gleaned from the best of the tradition, as transposed to our new world in which social and psychological analysis shed light on nonviolent transformations of individual and communal life (chapter six). Again, examples of contemporary persons in their contexts illustrate the variety of ways in which lives and communities are transformed—atonement at work in concrete journeys over time.

The positions taken in this book retain an orthodoxy grounded in theologies of Incarnation and the Trinity, as defined by Nicea and Chalcedon, along with positions elucidated by Irenaeus, Augustine, and Anselm. At the same time, I aim not merely to repeat language from a previous era but to bring basic positions on Christ and atonement into the modern age. This work depends on a distinction among different "realms of meaning": that of common sense, theoretical explanation, and interiority analysis. Among other things I conclude that atonement theology is not to be conceived of as a transaction, either between humankind and God, or between different persons of the Trinity. Rather, it has to do with a dramatic shift in one's horizon of meaning; the kingdom of God as Jesus describes it and the new life of resurrection that Paul emphasizes. Because this new life involves a dramatic reversal of meanings, it lacks any kind of logic or direct chain of causality. Likewise, it does not come about through force or coercion; it is a conversion that comes as a gratuitous act of God with which we can cooperate or not. Furthermore, atonement is not something that happened in the distant past. It is ongoing as the Spirit of resurrection works in individual and communal lives. Finally, the only true way to verify this interpretation is for the reader to recognize the elements that I present and identify them in his or her own life and that of their community.

*the journey*

*The journey is atonement*

# 1

# Falling in Love

## Healing and Reconciliation Enfolded in God's Embrace

We have seen the problems that some of the standard accounts of salvation—in the language of redemption, atonement, sacrifice—have yielded, particularly for the contemporary believer repelled by the proliferation of violence and abuse, especially as propagated in and through religious practices and institutions.

Nevertheless, persons continue to live faithful lives and many find radically renewed lives in Christ. Let us look in this chapter at how lives are changed through encounters with God, and specifically through a relationship with Jesus Christ, encompassed by the Holy Spirit. Here we will give a generic, commonsense account of the human person, his or her need for God, and a lifetime journey of death and resurrection as part of a community of faith. The details of how this unfolds in any particular life in its concrete context need to be added. A few examples are given at the end of the chapter, but each reader can add his or her own specifics. How all this fits within the Christian tradition that we have inherited and how we might explain it in a more analytic way today will come in later chapters.

# A Life of Death and Resurrection

The first thing to note about our current context is that we now understand "salvation" or "atonement"—the making-us-right-with-God—as a *process* not a *state of being*. This is part of a bigger historical shift in modern consciousness—which we will explain later—but for now we will begin discussing the human person in terms of the life cycle.

## *Being Human*

As infants we are mostly taken up with animal instincts and needs. This includes not only the need for food, water, and someone to change our diapers, but the need for touch—cuddling, holding, caressing—and other kinds of stimulation. Hence, we now recognize the importance of early attachment to caregivers, and the power of modeling and imitation at critical stages of childhood. Yet right from the start, human infants have another quality: the ability to *wonder*. Our bonding with caregivers includes sounds and sights that stimulate attention and, eventually, inquiry. From the beginning, the tools for language are being put in place so that when we become toddlers the incessant "Why?" questions begin. Play and experimentation figure into this exploration of what is not us. This means that we all have the capacity to move beyond ourselves; to bond with others in meaningful ways, to trust our caregivers implicitly, to try on different roles in social interaction, to long to understand and conquer our worlds, however small or insignificant.

Thus it is the nature of being human both to go beyond our current realities and to be entrapped within them. We are fascinated—ever fascinated—with the other, with the world around us. An aspect of this interest is of course *self*-interest, yet its reach beyond ourselves is unlimited. There is always more to experience, more to try and to understand, more to affect with our actions. Still, we are stuck in a body, a time, and a place. We do need to eat and poop and get some sleep. So we are—forever—a contradiction; captivated by unrestricted wonder yet limited in our reach, both literally and figuratively.

We also are all born into an already constituted community. Biologically we are conceived through some relationship, whether it involves romance, licentious sex, or a petri dish. No one comes alone into the world. Whether wealthy or poor, from an upper middle-class American suburb or a refugee camp in Lebanon, none of us is a blank slate. We are born into a world of *meaning* and *value*. We inherit these meanings and these values and they affect us from the very moment we are brought into life, if not before.

So our needs and our wonder are shaped initially by others. These others find themselves in worlds defined by still others, not only other individuals but other social structures, social institutions, economic frameworks. A child born in a refugee camp in Turkey in 2014 is conditioned, from the beginning, in a very different way than a child born in 1966 in a commune in San Francisco.

These preestablished meanings and values then come to shape our wonder and our needs. Our needs are met—or not—laden with narratives about who we are, to whom we belong, which needs are legitimate and when and how they should be met. Our wonder is met with answers; we are told what is true, we are given explanations to make sense of these truths, we receive hints about what counts and what doesn't. In the process our very experiencing is shaped: our seeing, our hearing, our paying attention, our feelings of excitement or shame.

What becomes most significant is the way our needs and our wonder themselves are interpreted. If meeting my needs is understood to be optimal (in other words, I am spoiled), I will inherit a particular set of expectations. If, on the other hand, I am punished for being hungry, or having a dirty diaper, my expectations of life and of myself will be diminished. Likewise, if my inexhaustible wonder is encouraged, even if my world is resource-poor, I will have a sense of my own capabilities that will support my native tendency to marvel.

Accordingly, not only am I as an individual a combination of constructive creativity and very real limitations, so also is my community. The strengths of a tradition lie in its role in protecting infants and guiding child development. A community's meanings and values take natural inquisitiveness and orient it, providing the curious child with tools to negotiate her questions about and interactions with the world around her. The liability of communal life and the power of social persuasion is that dramatically negative influences can affect very malleable hearts and minds toward distorted feelings and ideas. As mentioned above, these are most destructive when they involve messages about our creativity and embodiment themselves.

So we come to what the Judeo-Christian tradition has designated as *sin*. This is the recognition that the human spirit, while itself oriented beyond itself, can become mired in self-indulgence in a way that curtails this orientation to the good. Ironically, there is a way in which the distortion of this native goodness lies in its unrestricted nature. Because our imaginations and our questions reach to the sky, so to speak, we can think that we ourselves have no limits. We mistake our urge for comprehensive knowledge with the reality of such knowledge. We erroneously think we are gods. Or we simply assume that our ideas and needs and pleasures and urges take precedence over everyone else's, that we deserve special attention as if we were gods.

The author of the book of Genesis gets at this aspect of human nature in the third chapter—the story of Adam and Eve in the garden. This is the stuff of "mythos," of story told as events that serve as commentary on the nature of the cosmos. In this case, it is the heart of human nature and its stubborn propensity to overreach itself that is at stake. While a surface reading interprets the essence of Adam and Eve's sin as disobedience, there is something deeper at work here. It is the temptation to be like God—knowing good and evil—that so captures our iconic forbearers. The story is not about some literally existent parents of the human race but is about each and every one of us. We are all tempted to overreach ourselves and do what we can to become like gods.

But the dilemma does not remain merely at the individual level. The disorientation that comes with the basic sin of self-aggrandizement has its social consequences, as the further chapters in Genesis illustrate. Power and shame are perpetuated; jealousy and rancor are passed on from one generation to another. So while sin is, at root, a failure to accept our limitations while yielding to the wonder that moves us beyond ourselves, the effects of these failures become entrenched in cultural mores and social systems.

Social sin is the systemic evil that keeps certain persons disenfranchised while elevating others to privileged status. It involves practices that disregard the earth's natural systems and the impact of human affairs on those systems. It affects not just structures like an economy, but penetrates to the very consciousness of whole social classes.[1] The very way one is aware of one's world, the way one pays attention, the expectations one has of life, can become disordered. Thus, not only is it true that we come into the world already influenced by the meanings and values of a community, those meanings and values are skewed by generations of individual and group biases. Social prejudices and the assumption that "man" can manipulate "nature" at will permeate our cultures.

This distortion is what we traditionally have called original sin, and its fruit is a social "surd" in which reasonable and good persons who choose reasonable and good courses of action are less and less numerous. This results in a moral impotence in which the course of human affairs—writ large or small—gets stuck in cycles of decline. As Bernard Lonergan puts it:

> There is no use appealing to the sense of responsibility of irresponsible people, to the reasonableness of people that are unreasonable, to the intelligence of people who have chosen to be obtuse, to the attention of people that attend only to their own grievances. Again, the objective situation brought about by sustained unauthenticity is not an intelligible situation. It is the product of inattention, obtuseness, unreasonableness, irresponsibility. It is an objective surd, the realization of the irrational.[2]

We are each, thus, a combination of a great eros of the human spirit reaching beyond ourselves to truth, beauty, and value, and the very mitigated reach of our embodied spirits. This limitation is due both to our finitude as creatures and to the sinful social structures in which we grow and develop. It is also due to the choices we make. Sin is both what I receive and what I create. I am subject to the social sin that comes before

---

1 On social sin and its several dimensions, see Gregory Baum, *Religion and Alienation: A Theological Reading of Sociology* (New York: Paulist Press, 1975), esp. pp. 197–213.

2 Bernard J. F. Lonergan, "Dialectic of Authority," in *A Third Collection*, ed. Frederick E. Crowe (New York: Paulist Press, 1985), 9.

me and influences me. But I am also responsible for the choices I make within the concrete reality in which I live. Either way, both I and my culture are stuck in the moral impotence whereby the actions we take to solve the problems created by sin only perpetuate them. As St. Paul puts it:

> I do not understand my own actions. For I do not do what I want, but I do the very thing I hate. . . . For I do not do the good I want, but the evil I do not want is what I do. Now if I do what I do not want, it is no longer I that do it, but the sin that dwells within me. So I find it to be a law that when I want to do what is good, evil lies close at hand. For I delight in the law of God in my inmost self, but I see in my members another law at war with the law of my mind, making me captive to the law of sin that dwells in my members. Wretched man that I am! Who will rescue me from this body of death? (Rom. 7:15,19–24)

Moral impotence in the inner person involves this struggle and failure to do what we most desire. Moral impotence reveals itself at the sociocultural level as the surd whereby reason fails to make its case since people are unreasonable, and the good cannot be discerned because the discerners are themselves prejudiced. How can we turn a situation around if even our understandings of the situation are distorted by our dysfunctional psyches? How does new vision and new life emerge if even our deepest desires are disordered in determining the good?

## Turning Moral Impotence Around

Concretely, what happens in some people's lives is that we fall in love and this falling in love changes everything. It could be the love of parent and child, of romantic partners committed to the long haul, of lifelong friends. The love given and received, not as fleeting emotions but as an undertow carrying everything forward, transforms our lives from self-service to self-sacrifice. "Besides particular acts of loving, there is the prior state of being in love, and that prior state is, as it were, the fount of all one's actions. So mutual love is the intertwining of two lives. It transforms an "I" and "thou" into a "we" so intimate, so secure, so permanent, that each attends, imagines, thinks, plans, feels, speaks, acts in concern for both."[3] This undertow of love propels us to seek truth when deceit is rife, to promote values that will enhance the flourishing of our loved ones, to speak out for justice when power has triumphed over the good.

Furthermore, for some of us this experience of love goes beyond the human to the "transcendent," the "wholly other." In other words, we fall in love with something beyond our creaturely existence. Bernard Lonergan calls it an "otherworldly falling in love"; Paul Tillich calls it "being grasped by ultimate concern"; and Rudolph Otto speaks of the *mysterium fascinans et tremendum* (fearful and fascinating mystery).[4] This religious experience, like all of human life and meaning, begins very simply in childhood and grows and changes over a lifetime. It involves the deep level of our lives that defies explanation or expression. It catapults our concern for others beyond our inner circle of kin and compatriots to a wider vision that includes all human persons and creation itself in its many manifestations.

For those in the Christian tradition, this Other with whom we fall in love is not just a creative force field but a person. We inherit from the Jewish tradition not only a robust view of God as an all-powerful creator but also a notion of God as engaged in history and in relationship with human persons. This is both a majestically awesome God and a lovingly present one, a God who establishes a covenant with Israel and faithfully follows her through apostasy and infidelity. This God provides his people with the Torah—the Law—as a means of preserving and nurturing the covenant relationship.

Christians believe that this awesome and faithful God entered history in a particular way in the life, death, and resurrection of Jesus of Nazareth. In addition to the "inner word" involved in the otherworldly falling-in-love mentioned above, there is the "outer word" of a person in history who supremely revealed God to humankind. In fact, as Christians we believe that this historical person was God himself. Furthermore, after his death and resurrection, the risen Christ returned to the Father

---

3 Bernard Lonergan, *Method in Theology* (New York: Seabury Press, 1972), 33.

4 Ibid., 106. See Paul Tillich, *Dynamics of Faith* (New York: Harper Collins, 1957) and Rudolf Otto, *The Idea of the Holy* (London: Oxford University Press, 1923).

and a new era emerged; the Holy Spirit that had raised Jesus from death was sent anew into the world to be ever-present with the community of disciples that came to be called "Christians."

The point here is not to begin delineating Christian dogma, but to note that the fascination with the *mysterium tremendum* that constitutes religious experience is, for Christians, an experience of *relationship.* Indeed, it is a threefold relationship, with a nurturing Father/Mother, a risen Lord who lived concretely in history, and the Spirit that permeates all of creation and promotes the reversal of sin and decline in our lives today. We enter into the love that exists within God in Godself, and experience this love over and over again as our lives unfold.

How does this concretely operate in Christians' lives? While the specific ways in which we are met by this incomprehensible love-made-incarnate are as manifold as there are persons and circumstances, we can say a few things in general about how this loving relationship goes forward.[5]

We may be socialized into the Christian tradition in a way that captivates our deepest desires and stimulates our imaginations. So we are provided with a treasure trove of stories, images, and personal narratives that ever propel us forward in living out our deep longing for the "more" beyond our small world of minor concerns. Alternately, we may have been raised into a religious tradition that so stifled our deepest yearnings, and/or promoted such a terrifying or restrictive view of God that our psyches were severely damaged. Or we may have had no religious training as children yet been encouraged in our curiosity to always seek truth, beauty, and goodness.

Whatever our socialization, at some point we are touched by the "numinous," a sense of something beyond us that captures our hearts and minds and pushes us to learn more. Dorothy Day was an atheist and anarchist. When she became pregnant, she was so enthralled by the miracle of life growing within her that she concluded there must be a

---

5  This account, admittedly, presumes a lifestyle in which basic needs are more or less taken care of. In other words, it describes the general frame of reference of persons who have enough to eat each day, who have access to good educational systems, who look forward to growing into lives of contribution to society. It does not seek to describe the lives of those in deep poverty or who live in dangerous political and social circumstances. Clearly, God's love is experienced in such situations and there are extraordinary examples of how God has worked in them. This description serves only as a model that of course needs to be applied and amended to fit diverse contexts and stories.

God and she decided to learn more about this Creator. C. S. Lewis was engaged for years in intellectual questions about atheism and the existence of God; then one day he got on a bus at the bottom of a hill and when he got off at the top he simply knew that God existed. In both these cases there was a long journey of learning more about this God they had encountered, specifically as known in Jesus Christ, but the initial encounter came as a gift unforeseen. Hmm...

This experience of gift—the fact that encounters between God and our deeper selves comes not as a matter of achievement but as an unheralded offering—is at the core of many believers' lives. We can undertake disciplines of prayer, worship, or Bible study, but the relationship we have with God is not something that we can manipulate or control. In fact, the idea that our faith is a matter of God's action upon us rather than the other way around is what Christians call "grace" and it has been at the heart of Christian lives from the earliest disciples on down through history. God comes to us, in all our concreteness and brokenness, and we respond.

What about this brokenness, the sinful selves and structures in which we are stuck without obvious resolution? How does this gift of encounter and otherworldly falling-in-love change any of the moral impotence and destruction in our lives or in the world? Does a single encounter with the numinous magically change people from sinners to saints?

While love as expressed and experienced in ongoing encounters with God has a transformative effect, this occurs within long journeys of pain, struggle, and renewal. We, and our worlds of meaning and value, are broken and there is no easy fix. So we as individuals and as communities of faith enter into the story of Jesus's life, death, and resurrection, not as an event long ago but as made new daily in our concrete lives. We put ourselves into the stories of Jesus's life and teaching and thereby immerse ourselves in his countercultural message. As much as we are able, we put into practice his teachings about the kingdom of God. This involves us in our own countercultural actions, combating our personal addictions and prejudices while serving those marginalized from social benefits. We seek out those who are victims of injustice and seek to reorient structures that mitigate against full human flourishing.

But the Jesus story is about so much more than moral injunctions or ethical imitation. The story is about a Messiah who is risen from the dead, who is present still today in our midst through the Holy Spirit. So we immerse ourselves in his story in order to grow in divine relationship within a present reality. Part of that story and our reality is the power of evil to infiltrate human minds and hearts and social systems. And the apex of the Jesus story is the utter failure of Jesus's human mission and the complete victory of ill-meaning power-hungry authorities. In this we identify with Jesus to the extent that we have been broken by those wielding power over us as well as in the ways in which we have participated in a life of power-brokering ourselves. Jesus lived his life to the full, in communion with God the Father and the Holy Spirit. His love was manifest in his willingness to die rather than perpetuate evil systems by striking back at his detractors. In entering this story over and over again we discover and rediscover ourselves as both victims and sinners. At the same time we encounter Christ's great love in choosing to suffer evil rather than perpetuate it.

The heart of the story is, of course, not the crucifixion by itself but the empty tomb discovered three days later. This is the heart of the story for Christians today as well. Our "other-worldly falling-in-love" comes to ground concretely where our lives of brokenness and deceit are revealed and thus reversed. This is the work of God in our lives—the graced moments of both grief and great joy when we face our wounds and our sins in light of God's perpetual healing and forgiving love. Many many things may facilitate these recurrent renewals: the love of others in a worshiping community of faith, worship itself in all its manifestations, from song to smell to sacrament. Study and intellectual pursuit aid some, immersion in the natural world speaks to others. Long periods of silent prayer or verbal praying in tongues—God's grace comes to us in varied and multiple manners.

## Multiple Conversions

Through the life cycle, our recurrent religious conversions shift and change in their focus. When we move from being young children to adolescents, we naturally move from literal pleasure and pain concerns to more intangible needs for social approval and security. As we negotiate our identities as teenagers—over against both our parental guardians and our peers—God often comes as an intimate companion affirming us in our uniqueness. The love of God—both for God and from God—captures our energy and exuberance and gives us a place in our social worlds. The wonderful feeling of being loved by an Other right down to our core carries the day. Jesus becomes a cherished friend and confidante, the Holy Spirit a vehicle by which we experience the Father's nurturing love. This powerful affective bond can propel the young faithful to energetic and courageous works of mercy: mission trips, work in underprivileged communities, new ventures to bring hope to forgotten parts of society. Any church community is enhanced by such passion.

As we get older and life gets more complicated, the initial exuberance can wane. Alternately, we can cling to the good feelings of our first godly infatuation, presuming that feeling good about God is the same as being in God's presence. As in any love relationship, if it is to last, the focus must shift from the more fleeting moments of exhilaration to the deeper undertow of committed love. We also come to discover some of the more negative sides of ourselves and our situations. We grow to be disillusioned with our anticipations of life. The systemic inequities of our society become apparent. Marriages turn out to be based on social mores or false promises that don't pan out. A career may falter. Family expectations may land us in jobs we don't want. We start to realize that roles set out for us due to social class or gender or assumptions about sexual orientation are faulty.

So our participation in the Jesus narrative also begins to shift. Rather than resurrection serving as a panacea that makes everything in my life and my world perfect, just like I want it to be, it turns out there are multiple deaths and resurrections to be lived through. We come face-to-face with some of the inherited distortions from our personal or social traditions. Most painfully, we can discover that our religious traditions themselves have dysfunctional elements. Sometimes, in order to follow the deepest desires of our hearts, to pursue the wonder that reaches to the truly transcendent, we need to reject or leave our religious homes. We are called to discover a path that is truly God's call for us, not that prescribed by others, however well intentioned.

This further move has been spoken of as a conversion "from religion to God." The outer trappings of religious practice become refined as we begin to distinguish the institutions that have nurtured us from the ground of God's love. We move from the joys of the "baptism of water" to the more difficult "baptism by blood." While this latter term has its origins in the martyrs of the early Christian centuries, we all enter into a martyrdom of sorts as our false selves erode and new psychic and social infrastructures emerge. Spiritual guides have also referred to this as a stage of "purgation," in which our sinful habits and dysfunctional defenses are purged, just like a special diet might purge our bodies of toxins.[6] Because it can involve moving beyond conventional religion, we can experience this as a kind of loss of faith, or a time of spiritual darkness.[7]

If we persevere in this darkness, we discover that our relationship with God has moved into a new mode. Rather than thinking in terms of faithfulness that will be rewarded, or a life that will issue into complete freedom and happiness, we discover that there is a kind of darkness that is part of life itself. That is to say, we encounter our limitations again. Not only are we limited by our bodies and our locus in a time and a place but the reach of our wonder and knowledge are finite. The beginning of wisdom is to know that we don't know. Rather than expecting that one day the darkness will end and be replaced by multiple lightbulbs of insight, we grow more comfortable in the "not-knowing-ness." This is often accompanied, as we grow older, with the restrictions imposed by changing bodies and intermittent or even life-threatening health concerns.

The centerpiece of this growth in faith is the ever-constant cycle of death and resurrection. While a confrontation with physical death may be part of our story, there is the ongoing challenge of our deep desires and their limitless reach toward truth, beauty, and love combined with

---

6 On traditions with regard to stages on the spiritual journey, see Jean Marc LaPorte, "Understanding the Spiritual Journey: From the Classical Tradition to the Spiritual Exercises of Ignatius," at http://www.jesuits.ca/orientations/stages%20in%20the%20 spiritual%20journey.pdf. Accessed May 23, 2015.

7 For a psychological perspective on the development of faith, see James W. Fowler, *Stages of Faith: The Psychology of Human Development and the Quest for Meaning* (San Francisco: Harper & Row, 1981), and Fowler, *Becoming Adult, Becoming Christian: Adult Development and Christian Faith* (San Francisco: Harper & Row, 1984). On the dark night of the soul, see Constance Fitzgerald, "Impasse and Dark Night," in *Women's Spirituality: Resources for Christian Development*, 2nd ed., ed. Joanne Wolski Conn (New York, Paulist Press, 1996), 410–35.); Barbara Dent, *My Only Friend Is Darkness: Living the Night of Faith with St. John of the Cross* (Washington, DC: ICS Publications, 1992), and Gerald May, MD, *The Dark Night of the Soul: A Psychiatrist Explores the Connection between Darkness and Spiritual Growth* (San Francisco: Harper San Fransciso, 2005).

our very partial successes in satisfying such desires. God comes to us, over and over again, with an experienced fulfillment of these desires even and especially when we ourselves can't reach up to them. Our sins, our wounds, our social realities, and our mere creatureliness curtail our flourishing. Yet God provides such flourishing in ever surprising ways and through various and serendipitous means. Gradually we move from contract thinking—God will give us what we want if we do things right—to covenant love—an adventure of trust in relationship to the divine.

What does "redemption" or "salvation" or "atonement" mean in this picture of faith? As indicated earlier, it is not a matter of attaining something or reaching a "state" of grace in God's eyes. Rather it is this ongoing adventure in relationship in which we perpetually enter and reenter the Jesus story of death and resurrection as part of our own dying to self. Jesus of Nazareth is also the risen Lord of the Church. In the cycles of the church year we put ourselves into his birth, life, death, and resurrection and discover our sins and our need for healing over and over again. We die and are reborn many times over and so live a journey of atonement. The Holy Spirit meets us in this as an always-present companion who gradually touches our hearts and changes our desires. Gently, over time, with plenty of messiness and struggle, sometimes requiring great courage, our deepest desires for the truly "beyond" replace our minor but persistent idolatries.[8]

This growth in love and identification with the crucified and risen Lord is often accompanied by a growing identification with others in their struggles. Whether it is members of our own family, neighbors down the street, or women and children kept against their will in human trafficking circles (who may, surprisingly, actually *be* down the street), we—forgiven and healed ourselves—become agents of change for others. So not only do we receive God's forgiveness and love, we incarnate saving help ourselves. God uses us in our frailty to be a means of grace for others. These others, in turn, are much more than the recipients of charity; they serve as agents of divine love for us as well.

However mature or spiritually wise we are, this process of living

---

8 For more on this approach to salvation, see Sebastian Moore, *Jesus: Liberator of Desire* (New York: Crossroad, 1989). See also Sebastian Moore, *The Contagion of Jesus: Doing Theology As If It Mattered* (Maryknoll, NY: Orbis Books, 2007).

in the dark dependent on God's grace, the cycles of dying, rising, and dying again, are unending. They will go on right up until our physical death. We do hope for a complete fulfillment of our longing for God beyond death. This hope of future realization is writ throughout the New Testament and was heralded in the medieval tradition as the "beatific vision," when we will see God face-to-face. But we can barely imagine what this existence will be like, except that it will be a continuation and intensification of the divine love we experience in the here and now. In any case, our lives of covenant love in the here and now—our salvation—will never cease to revolve through death and new life.

# Sample of Lives Lived in Faith

Having presented a description of Christian faith as a process of salvation in general terms, let us provide a few case studies to illustrate how this appears when some "flesh" is added. These are composite and fictional personages and provide mere glimpses into lives of faith, but they offer some illustrations that can fill out the broad account given above.

## Clarissa

Clarissa is the daughter of Italian immigrants to the United States. Her father, Francesco, came to the United States when he was eighteen years old and found work in the mines of Western Pennsylvania. He met a young woman from northern Italy who had emigrated with her parents when she was eleven, settling in the same town where Francesco worked. They married and had four children, of which Clarissa was the oldest. Clarissa grew up as a student in the local and very traditional Roman Catholic school in her district, attending church regularly. Her mother worked from home as a seamstress and attended mass every day. Clarissa's first communion, just prior to the changes that came with Vatican II, was a major feast in the community, complete with white gloves, white dresses, and much fanfare.

When Clarissa was eleven, she was chosen to help decorate the church for special occasions, along with several other girls from her school. She felt quite privileged to do this and loved making their little parish church as beautiful as possible. On a few occasions, the priest asked her to stay after the others had gone home. She again felt quite privileged and was especially pleased to have a special relationship with Father Roger, whom she admired. Mostly they had chats about her life in school and her family. At one point Father Roger asked her to sit on his lap so they could be more comfortable while they talked. At first she thought this was odd, but then it became routine. Eventually, Father Roger began holding her in ways she did not like, and touching private parts of her body. He assured her that this was normal. Though it made her feel quite uncomfortable and she asked him to stop, she had no way to avoid these encounters. The one or two times she tried to talk about this with her mother, she was silenced and accused of being disrespectful.

At the age of eighteen Clarissa was fortunate enough to receive a scholarship to John Carroll University in Cleveland, where she received a degree in education. She participated in the campus ministry at the school and enjoyed the very progressive liturgies that were held. She grew in her faith and helped to begin a praise and worship service that took place each Sunday evening. She was able to use her musical talents to assist in these services by playing the piano. She met and married Paul, a fellow student and a devout Catholic.

Clarissa and Paul both were able to get jobs in a big city not far from Clarissa's parents. Clarissa taught high school science while Paul worked in a church-based mission that served the homeless. Though they attended their local parish, they were not comfortable with the priest, who was resistant to the changes that had come with Vatican II. Problems developed in the marriage due to Paul's increasing drinking habits and Clarissa's discomfort with their sexual lives. When Clarissa approached her priest for help, he dismissed her concerns as "infantile" and told her that her job was to please her husband. Paul pressed her to have children and chided her on her "issues" when it came to sexual intimacy.

Eventually, the couple split up and after several years divorced. Clarissa's mother was ashamed and Clarissa left the church altogether. She did not attend church for over a decade. By her mid-thirties she had advanced to being a vice principal in a publically funded middle school. She was offered a job as principal in a very prestigious Catholic girls school. While she very much wanted the job, she realized that if she took it, she would have to come to terms with her past. In the end she took the job but also entered into therapy and found a companion in her journey in a close female friend who was a Presbyterian minister. It was only through therapy and this friend's encouragement that Clarissa came to recognize that she had been sexually abused. The next year she committed herself to a Lenten journey that involved exploring her religious heritage and writing a spiritual autobiography. She attended the Easter vigil that year, the first in over ten years, and was brought to tears with both grief and joy as the darkness turned to light and "Jesus has risen" was heralded by choir and organ together.

Clarissa has become an active member of her local Roman Catholic church. She has remarried and, while unable to have biological children, she and her husband adopted a young boy from China, and four years later a baby from Peru. She has become enthralled with concerns over the environment and left the educational field to start a foundation that promotes urban gardening. She continues to make annual retreats and has an active prayer life. She has a deep love for Jesus and a growing sense of the Creator blessing her each day.

## Gerald

Gerald is an Augustinian monk in his eighties who lives in a monastery just outside Toronto. He was raised as a Catholic in Nova Scotia, where his German ancestors had settled. He always loved the church and had a childhood devotion to the sacred heart of Jesus. He attended Catholic schools and found a mentor in a beloved uncle who was an Augustinian. When an opportunity came to attend an Augustinian high school in Toronto, Gerald jumped at the chance. Shortly after his graduation, he followed his uncle's example and entered the Augustinians as a novice in Halifax.

As part of his novitiate, he attended university and studied English literature. Upon completing his degree and his novitiate, he took final vows and began working at a parish school in rural Nova Scotia. Over time, he began to find the work both tedious and boring. Life in community felt harsh; in the pre–Vatican II days there was a great emphasis on abnegation and self-discipline. Gerald began to lose his love for life and to question why he had undertaken such a joyless vocation. At the age of thirty, his superior noticed his lethargy and asked him if he would consider further study. Although Gerald had not been thinking of more schooling, he believed a change would be good for him. The Augustinians felt they needed someone trained in biblical studies and so sent him off to the University of St. Michael's College in Toronto to get a PhD in New Testament studies.

To his surprise, Gerald loved studying the New Testament. The winds of change were beginning to blow in relation to biblical studies in the Roman Catholic Church. By the time *Dei Verbum* (Word of God) was issued by the Second Vatican Council in the fall of 1965, Gerald had completed his doctorate and joined a growing cadre of new Roman Catholic biblical scholars. His personal spiritual life changed dramatically with his work on St. Paul and the book of Romans. There he discovered a theological idea that was new to him—that his salvation depended solely on God's work in Christ. It was a gift of love, a grace given that he received in a new way. The idea that God was always at work, drawing him closer, relieved Gerald of a sense of burden in his religious life.

This renewed perspective on faith energized Gerald in his ministry. He was sent to teach at a high school—his alma mater—in Toronto, specifically to teach young minds about the Bible. He jumped into this work eagerly and spent over four decades teaching Bible while developing his own new interests in biblical scholarship. Among other things, in the 1970s Gerald got involved in the charismatic movement as it swept through Roman Catholic communities in Toronto. His new regard for the work of the Holy Spirit changed both his ministry with teenagers and his studies. He undertook new research about the Holy Spirit in the New Testament and became an expert in this area of scholarship.

At the age of seventy-five Gerald stepped down from his teaching role at the high school. In retirement he has undertaken a new ministry with veterans at the Sunnybrook healthcare center in Toronto, leading Sunday liturgies and offering pastoral care, when needed, to the long-term care residents. His own prayer life has become one of quiet contemplation and he finds that he is happy to spend several hours a day reading his Bible and praying.

## *Sarah*

Sarah is forty years old and lives in St. Louis, Missouri. She grew up in Seattle, Washington, in a family that had no particular religious affiliation. Until the age of eleven she had never attended church. At that age the man who lived next door—Tom Martin—developed prostate cancer. Along with various treatments, Tom and his family undertook a series of prayer meetings in their living room, to pray specifically for his healing. The Martins invited Sarah's family to join them each week. More out of curiosity than any kind of faith, Sarah, her brothers, and her parents went to this prayer gathering every Sunday evening for over six months.

After this six months, Tom Martin passed away. His family handled his death with grace and continued to invite Sarah's family over for fellowship. Eventually, Sarah's whole family was baptized and began attending a Pentecostal church along with the Martins. Sarah eagerly participated in youth Bible studies and spent five summers at a church camp, where her faith deepened. When she moved to St. Louis after college, she found a Pentecostal church to her liking and remains a regular attendee to this day.

Sarah has had a number of career interests, mostly in paralegal fields. At the age of thirty-two, she had an opportunity to become a death row investigator for the state of Missouri. This is a job that involves cases in which persons sentenced to death are appealing their sentences. It is Sarah's job to undertake a neutral investigation to determine the facts about the case and whether there is any warrant for its reexamination. In the process she gets to know the inmates in some depth, exploring not only what happened on a given day in the past, but how it was that he or she came to commit a crime. Sarah also interviews and gets to know the families of victims of these crimes.

While Sarah is neither a social worker nor an advocate, she became quite enchanted with the stories of those on death row. The more she began to investigate, the more she was struck by the humanity of those who awaited execution. Many of them had to wait in suspense to find out if their cases would be heard again. Even if it seemed clear that there was no reprieve in sight, some had to wait for years for an execution date to be set. Sarah found many of them nevertheless to live with joy and curiosity, eager to read or paint or sew or converse or do whatever they could to make their time worthwhile.

This work added a great deal of substance to Sarah's faith. She is not naïve about the crimes committed nor the prospect of complete reform for those she interviews. But her work has given her a new sense of the humanity of everyone and she feels called to bring this humanity to light. She believes it is a God-given humanity that should not be denigrated no matter what the circumstances.

At the age of thirty-eight, a never-married single, Sarah has undertaken two new tasks. She has adopted two children from the social services in St. Louis—Jeremy who is three and Karen who is five—and has begun a writing project for inmates on death row. She encourages those on death row to write their autobiographies and she has found editors willing to help them craft their stories into publishable form. She is developing a network of publishers who are interested in bringing these stories to light. At the same time, she is developing parenting support groups to help her with her new family. Her church, her parents, and her brothers are enthusiastic about both new ventures and offer financial and emotional assistance.

## Mathias

Mathias is a seventy-year-old father, grandfather and great-grandfather who lives in a village just outside Dodoma, the capital of Tanzania. He has been a faithful Anglican all his life, having attended an Anglican school when he was a child. He speaks impeccable English and jokes about the "Queen's English" and his Oxford accent. He remembers the days of colonialism when everyone aspired to imitate the British.

Mathias works as an administrator at a medical dispensary in Dodoma, walking a half hour each way to and from the bus stop in order to take the bus into the city. He and his wife of forty years live in a mud brick house on the edge of town. They have intermittent electricity and cook outside on charcoal. They are fortunate to have had the funds to put a well in their yard. Neighbors come to get water and leave them coins to pay for it. They have a well-kept pit toilet in their side yard, several goats, and half a dozen chickens.

Mathias and his wife have five children, most of whom live nearby. His one son, Emmanuel, became quite successful as a businessman in Dar es Salaam. He bought a parcel of land on the other side of Dodoma, where he intended to build his parents a retirement home. This home, and Emmanuel's support, were to enable Mathias to retire in a few years. Unfortunately, Emmanuel passed away suddenly from a heart attack at the age of forty-eight. This was not only a great blow emotionally to Mathias, it meant that his future was now uncertain.

Mathias has been a faithful churchgoer all his life. He is immensely supportive of his local parish, attends every service there, and assists at other outlying churches as needed. He gives a large portion of his income to the church and contributes to whatever needs arise in his community. His home is often the center of village gatherings and he is looked up to when disputes arise with neighbors. His faith permeates all he does, and his love for God is apparent whenever he speaks of God.

When Emmanuel died, Mathias was saddened yet grateful. He said, "God is good and gave me forty-eight years with my wonderful son." He was proud, he was glowing, he was gracious and grateful. When it comes to concerns over his old age, he trusts in God's providence: "God must have a reason for Emmanuel's death. I am sure God knows what he is doing."

## Sharon

Sharon is in her late fifties now, having grown up in Jackson, Mississippi, the third of three children in a middle-class family. Her family attended church regularly at a local Baptist congregation. They routinely went to a Wednesday night family fellowship hour. Here Sharon learned her Bible stories frontward and backward. When she was twelve, she committed her life to Christ and was baptized.

After high school, Sharon married her teenage sweetheart and began work as a bank teller. Her husband, Adam, worked as a truck driver and was gone for long periods of time. Sharon got pregnant soon after they were married and had Nathan when she was twenty. She continued to work at the bank while her mother helped take care of Nathan. Nevertheless, with Adam's long absences and the challenge of a little baby, Sharon fell into a deep depression. For so long she had been told that it was her sins that had made Jesus die on the cross; she simply assumed that her depression must be punishment of some kind. She tried and tried to be more cheerful, to stop being so selfish. But her depression just grew. When Adam announced that he had found a trucking company in Georgia that would offer him better benefits, she was frightened but hoped that the move would make her a better wife and mother.

In Georgia Sharon was able to be a stay-at-home mom. She made friends with some of the neighbor women and joined a Bible study at the nearest church. But her depression did not subside. She attended several weekends for "women of faith" that buoyed her up for a while. Still, the Bible studies emphasized sin and the need to overcome selfishness in order to become a beautiful woman of God. Each Easter Sharon would feel more and more guilty that she was letting God down, that her sinfulness caused Jesus so much suffering.

Then Sharon discovered that her husband was having an affair. When she confronted Adam, he did not deny it but insisted that it was her fault. Had she been a more attentive wife, he would not have needed to stray. He insisted on a speedy divorce and left her with little income, though, gratefully, she did not have to fight for custody of Nathan, who was now seven.

After a period of complete disorientation, Sharon found a government program that would allow her to attend a community college. She enrolled in a small school outside Atlanta and discovered that she loved learning. She passed with flying colors and moved on to a university that accepted her credits toward a bachelor's degree. Eventually she got a degree in occupational therapy and was able to support herself and Nathan on her salary. She grew to be quite delighted with her own inquisitive nature and her newfound freedom.

In the meantime she had begun attending a United Methodist Church that was progressive with regard to women's ministry. She joined the pastoral care team and made regular visits to homebound parishioners. She participated in a Bible study that examined the women of the Bible and she discovered that they were all women with great skills and incredible courage. She grew in her trust of her church community and her trust of herself. The church did not look down on her for being divorced or being a single mom. Instead, they welcomed her and created a carpool of retired persons who could bring Nathan home from after-school activities when she had to work.

After ten years of spiritual growth and formation at this church, Sharon decided it was time for a change. She had become so beloved as part of the pastoral care team that her pastor asked her to considered ordained ministry. Nathan was ready to leave for college himself, with a scholarship, and her parents had left her a nest egg that would support her while she went to seminary. She attended seminary in Atlanta and in the process met and married Tom, also divorced, who was himself preparing for ministry in the Methodist church. He was very supportive of her vocation and got along well with Nathan. He had grown daughters who took some time to warm up to Sharon. Sharon graduated from seminary a year before Tom, but eventually they were assigned to a circuit of country churches in eastern Tennessee. They have had a successful dual ministry ever since. Sharon's spirituality now is one of deep gratitude. She especially loves to work with women who need encouragement due to difficult circumstances.

## Conclusion

This is just a sampling of the kinds of people who have discovered a relationship with God and followed it through many life stages and circumstances. While their cultures, their ages, their roles in life, and their geographies differ, nonetheless each story involves some key elements.

All of these people have a *deep longing for God*. For some, this is initially a vague orientation to learn more or experience as much as life can offer. For all, it is a desire that shifts and changes as they grow older and face new challenges. Some have experienced times when this deep yearning was lost or forgotten. In all cases, there have been vehicles of grace by which this profound desire has been nurtured and channeled; people or institutions or jobs that opened up new horizons of meaning or presented new choices to be made.

Each life story reveals an *ongoing saga of death and resurrection*. As the life cycle moves forward, old battle wounds and failures continue to resurface, to be faced, healed, and forgiven. "Death" can be the loss of a loved one or the disillusionment of a lost lifestyle. In each case the person brings his or her own humanity into the process. Body, gender, temperament, age, sexuality, intelligence, family, and culture of origin— all constitute dimensions of these persons' identities as they are transformed. For each there is some false self that tempts and tantalizes him

*You can only know what you know at a time given time*    *"false" self or self that hasn't reached a more enlightened part of the journey*

or her toward remaining in a narrowed framework of meaning. This false self is challenged and changed in the perpetual dying and rising that makes up the life of a Christian disciple.

At the heart of this series of transformations is *a relationship with God*. The faith of these folks has not been primarily an assent to a list of dogmas. Rather it has been a sense of relationship with God, a rapport that shifts and changes along with life circumstance. At times the nurturing love of a parental God—Father/Mother—predominates. Other times Jesus as friend and compatriot comes to the fore. A bond with the Holy Spirit sometimes takes the lead. In the times of darkness or dying, this sense of divine connection can fade. With each renewal there is a growing maturity in relationship that emerges.

All of these people find themselves in *communities of faith*. Growth in divine relationship is tied into incarnate bonds in the church. These church groups vary widely in how they spend their time nurturing faith, which vehicles of grace they emphasize—Bible study or sacraments or support groups—but without such embodied communal sharing, none of these individuals would have grown in faith.

While some people were subjected to very destructive influences from religious groups, the flourishing that comes with trusting God depends on finding a healthy church family. These church families themselves are ever shifting but each personal journey through death to resurrection is nourished by a vigorous set of companions in the faith.

This communal life incorporates, in all the stories, both a life of *worship* and a life of *service*. Again, the styles of worship vary extensively—in venue, use of music, the centrality of sacraments, preaching style, leadership structure and approach. But some kind of worship, some way of acknowledging God's greatness and of offering thanks for God's grace, is central to any communal life of faith.

The same is true of a life of service. Worship condones outward movement. Communal nurturing of faith generates the desire to share love with others. All of these narratives illustrate people whose faithfulness to God produces a sense of call, a vocation to change the world in a way most suited to their talents and resources. Most of these folks would not see themselves as involved in particularly great missions, only as doing what needs to be done in a certain place and time. The love of God simply spurs them on to turn their abilities toward systems or individuals that need help. Service can mean prophetic witness as well as charitable acts. The point is that faith rarely stands still—it reaches out to others.

Finally, for each of these persons of faith, growth in maturity involves a move away from what we can call an "addiction to feelings" toward a *gentle acceptance of reality*. Deep, committed faithfulness comes with detachment, not in any destructive ascetic manner, but in a growing self-emptiness that is less and less dependent on feeling good about God. The deep undertow of love cultivates a quiet acceptance of whatever God offers, whether it is moments of bliss or what Ignatius of Loyola called "hard consolation." What matters is not happiness but joy, and there is recognition that joy may include sorrow and grief. Being in love with God is being embraced by God no matter what the circumstance. All that matters is abiding in God's presence.

These are all stories of *atonement*: the slow process involved in recognizing sin, both as sins committed and sins suffered, and finding its reversal in forgiveness and healing. They are stories of reconciliation, with others and with God. Atonement as outlined here may not fit with the image that we have of Jesus dying for our sins. In order to tie this life-cycle account with the resources of the Christian tradition, we need to examine carefully the ways in which earlier theologians and communities have understood this concept.

# 2

# Retrieving the
# Biblical Tradition
## Paul and Jesus

In the first chapter we considered how lives change when the love of God shifts the ground on which persons constitute their lives. We used contemporary language and told stories of people living in a variety of modern contexts. But how does any of this fit with the biblical view of atonement? The notion that Jesus died for our sins is embedded in the New Testament and there are many passages that can be called upon to endorse a penal substitutionary view of redemption—the idea that we deserve death because we are sinners and that Jesus suffered that death in our place. But does the biblical witness in fact support the worst caricatures of this view, the ones that implicate God as the agent of Jesus's death and, hence, a God of violence? A careful reading indicates that there is no one "biblical view of atonement" but a host of meanings applied to Jesus's death and resurrection. Further, understanding the context of the expected kingdom of God in first-century Judaism, as well as grasping the underpinnings of Jewish sacrificial practice, can resolve many false appropriations of the saving significance of Jesus's life, death, and resurrection.

The task of adequately examining the corpus of the New Testament in this regard is well beyond our capacity here. For this reason we will limit our discussion to Paul's theological motifs and what we can glean from the Gospels about the meaning that Jesus ascribed to his life and death. In a preliminary section we will discuss how the experience of the earliest Christians evolved into what we now call the New Testament. We will then examine what we might determine about Jesus's own understanding of his death, and then treat Paul's theology in his letters.

# The Experience of the Early Followers of Jesus

Let's begin with a few preliminary points about how "theology" itself emerged in the first century.[1] We begin with the *lived* experience of the earliest Christians, which moved from resurrection backward to the details of Jesus's life and teaching and not the other way around. No one would have bothered remembering what Jesus said or did if it had not changed his or her life dramatically. These dramatic life changes began with the challenge to follow Jesus before his death but came to a climax with the claim that Jesus was risen from the dead. A few women insisted that they had found an empty tomb when they went to embalm Jesus's body after the Sabbath. Others insisted that Jesus had appeared among them, either at the tomb or as they gathered together in mourning. He came not as a ghost but with a real live body that could talk and eat. The characters and the stories vary according to the Gospel that you read, but one thing seems clear: everything that is recorded or written about Jesus

---

1 Anselm of Canterbury spoke of theology as "faith seeking understanding." This chapter is meant to be a glimpse at the early Christian community seeking to understand its newfound faith. The point here is that faith—or religious experience and conviction—came first. Then the community had to make sense of it. The community's thoughts—or at least some of them—were articulated and preserved for us, in Paul's letters, in the Gospels, and in the other documents that constitute our New Testament.

the Christ is told *after* the resurrection and *in light of* the resurrection. Something very extra-ordinary had happened and it radically changed those impacted by it. It was not anything that Jewish or Gentile world-views of the time could easily accommodate.[2] In light of this, the ear-liest Christians had a lot of work to do just to make sense of what Jesus was all about. Everything he had said or done suddenly had nuances and overtones that his followers had not noticed at the time. They were com-pelled to explain, to interpret, to make intelligible—to themselves if not to those outside the community—the meaning of Jesus's teachings, his life, and most of all his death.

This latter concern, that Jesus had died, not a natural death but an ignominious execution, came to the fore. How were his disciples to make sense of such a tragedy? Given the resurrection and the ongoing pres-ence of the Holy Spirit in their midst, it seemed that God had been doing something all along. But it was not at all what they had expected. None of the Jewish messianic expectations at large at the time included any-thing close to what had actually happened to Jesus. That their lives had changed no one questioned. What it meant—how to tell the story and where God's plan fit in—had to be determined.

So, while we cannot know exactly what happened at the tomb or in the days after Jesus's crucifixion, we can assert confidently at least two things: (1) his disciples were dramatically changed because of their con-viction that Jesus had been raised from the dead and (2) Jesus's brutal death needed explaining, if indeed God was at work in the events they had lived.

A further element that played a role was the fact that many new "Christians" were themselves suffering for their faith. Whether they were Gentiles whose families did not understand their newfound faith, or Jewish followers who found themselves unwelcome in the local syn-agogues, the followers of Jesus were often at odds with their cultural worlds.[3] Remembering the events of Jesus's life meant identifying with the opposition he encountered and the suffering that he underwent.

---

2 On the continuity and discontinuity between Christian claims and the expectations of Judaism and the Greco-Roman world of the time, see Christopher Bryan, *The Resurrection of the Messiah* (Oxford: Oxford University Press, 2011), 9–41 (esp. 38–39) and 170.

3 These controversies are illustrated in the book of Acts.

Telling the story of Jesus's suffering infused the believers' lives with meaning and purpose: to follow Jesus meant to follow him to the cross.[4]

All of these facts about the early church and its theologizing point to another factor involved here—the pastoral context in which the meaning of Jesus's life, death, and resurrection developed. First and foremost, the energized Jesus followers *preached.* Their first "theologizing" came in the form of *kerygma*—the Greek word for proclamation. The radical transformation of their lives and communities catapulted them into proclaiming the good news of life in Christ and the presence of the Holy Spirit to everyone around them.[5] As such, the good news of Jesus the Christ spread quickly and widely in the Mediterranean basin. This meant that the missionary message had to adapt to a full range of cultural and geographical contexts. It did this long before there were letters among and between churches and their missionaries, and prior to any written account of Jesus's life.

In sum, early on in the life of what became "Christianity" there were multiple "Christianities," each having to make sense of the events of Jesus's life, particularly of his execution and the claims of his resurrection. *That* knowing the Christ as risen from the dead changed lives was never in doubt. Just *what it all meant,* and how to proclaim that meaning to divergent constituencies threw the early churches into thinking theologically "on their feet," so to speak.

Our access to this early oral process of theological creativity is limited. It lies in the written records that emerged over a fifty-year period (roughly 50 CE to 100 CE) and that required an even longer time (three centuries) to be regarded as "scripture."[6] And while the Gospels seem chronologically closest to the historical events, in fact the earliest evidence that we have of Christian life and faith come from Paul's letters.[7] In

---

4  This is especially clear in the second half of Mark's Gospel.

5  This also is illustrated by Luke's account of the early church in the book of Acts.

6  This process involved designating a "canon" (meaning a "rule") of books that were considered sacred and authoritative for Christians. For more on this process, see Bruce Metzger, *The Canon of the New Testament: Its Origin, Development, and Significance* (New York: Oxford University Press, 1987) and Harry Gambie, *The New Testament Canon: Its Making and Meaning* (Minneapolis: Fortress Press, 1985).

7  While Paul's name is attached to a range of books in the New Testament, the following are generally accepted as authentically authored by Paul: Romans, 1 and 2 Corinthians, Galatians, Philippians, 1 Thessalonians, and Philemon. Scholars differ on the dating of these but the generally accepted timeframe would be 55 CE (1 Thess.) to the late 50s (Rom.) or early 60s (Phil.).

fact, all of Paul's letters were composed before anyone considered writing a Gospel.[8]

With Paul's letters we get a snapshot of what we have been discussing above—a missionary at work trying to manage his various outposts of new believers. In particular, he was working hard to influence—sometimes through polemic against *other* Christian missionaries—how the meaning of the gospel was preached and lived.[9] All of this emerges out of community relations. Unfortunately, we only have one side of the conversations. At times Paul seems to be quoting his opponents or his converts, so we can more or less guess what they have said or asked. But most of the time we are only getting bits and pieces of the context to which Paul is speaking.

In addition, Paul himself is not a theologian in the systematic sense of the word. He engages in polemic more than careful argument (even in Romans, his only explicitly theological treatise). More often he uses images and metaphors to get his points across. And he mixes these metaphors freely. He can jump from one image to the next without logical explanation. We will review his ideas and creative theologizing in due course, but for now we need to recognize: (1) Paul is the earliest biblical source we have for grasping the meanings that early Christians made of Christ's work; (2) he works from his own experience of meeting the risen Lord on the road to Damascus; (3) he is a pastoral theologian—making theological sense of Christ as it impacts his converts' lives; and (4) while his overall message is coherent, he is not a systematic theologian; he uses different metaphors and images in different contexts to make his points.

The earliest Gospel we have (Mark) likely was composed around 70 CE, after Paul had died. Just as Paul was a theologian trying to make theological sense of the death and resurrection of Jesus, in specific places and for specific audiences, so each of the Gospels takes a slightly different

---

8 This is not to say that nothing in the Gospels is earlier than the letters. It is just to point out that the *written* witness begins with Paul. A robust oral tradition existed prior to the writing of the Gospels. Scholars speculate about the reasons why some persons finally undertook the writing of Gospel narratives. There seem to be three elements: the eyewitnesses to Jesus's ministry, death, and resurrection were dying, the return of Jesus had not occurred immediately as some had expected, and there was a need for "quality control": as preachers did their work they needed reliable sources to use, especially over against the directions that some missionaries were taking that seemed to overlook the concrete life of Jesus and his disciples.

9 See E. P. Sanders, *Paul: A Very Short Introduction* (Oxford: Oxford University Press, 1991).

approach, depending on where and to whom it is written. The Gospel writers had plenty of materials to work with—oral stories and perhaps early written documents—but had to arrange them into a coherent narrative that also interpreted the meaning of the events. This accounts for the differences in both details and themes in the four Gospels. At the same time a few common features can be noted: (1) All of the Gospels are overshadowed by the passion narratives—Jesus's arrest, death, and subsequent resurrection feature prominently in each Gospel; (2) all the events of Jesus's ministry—his teachings and his actions—are interpreted in light of the resurrection and its wider cosmic, revelatory meaning; (3) the Gospel writers act as theologians, reflecting the already existing understandings of what God was doing in Jesus at the same time providing new angles of interpretation for their communities; and (4) in all cases the message has to do with how Jesus embodied the new way that God was working in and transforming the lives of believers, their communities, and indeed the whole world.

That the Gospel writers were all theological interpreters of the Jesus story is now evident and taken for granted. Just how well they reflect Jesus's own theological meanings and intentions remains a much-debated topic. This is often discussed as the question of the "Jesus of history" versus the "Christ of faith."[10] While the range of views spans from complete skepticism (we can't possibly know anything about Jesus in his historical reality) to utter conflation (there is no distinction between the Gospel accounts and what Jesus actually said or did), there is a strain of recent scholarship that seeks a middle way. That is to say, using good historical methods (not mere conjecture) we can infer what Jesus's life must have been like and understand the context of his teaching life, his death, and the earliest Christian witness. Within this contextual world of meaning there are some things we can say with confidence about what Jesus's message was and the impact it had on his followers.[11]

---

10 See N. T. Wright, *Jesus and the Victory of God* (Minneapolis: Fortress Press, 1996), chaps. 1–3 and John P. Meier, *A Marginal Jew: Rethinking the Historical Jesus*, 1st ed., 3 vols. (New York: Doubleday, 1991), vol. 1, chaps. 1 and 6.

11 See Peter Laughlin, *Jesus and the Cross: Necessity, Meaning, and Atonement*, Princeton Theological Monograph Series (Eugene OR: Pickwick Publishers, 2014), chap. 3.

# The Gospels and Jesus's
# Understanding of His Death

*[handwritten: The way she speaks of Jesus here makes him sound 100% human and 0% devine]*

Can we know what Jesus thought about his death? Given the fact that he saw himself in the prophetic tradition (and knew the fate of most prophets), that he knew what had happened to John the Baptist, and that he undertook provocative actions in the temple, it is safe to say that Jesus must have expected a premature death.[12] If that is the case, it is probable that he also had a set of meanings that he believed his death would invoke. What can we say about this? While a full account of Jesus's theology of his own death is not possible here, in fact may not be possible in any case, we can at least indicate a few elements that would have contributed to the sense Jesus made of his ministry and death. These fall into three categories: Jesus's whole project (what was he up to?), what Jesus said (his words), and Jesus's symbolic actions (in the temple and at the Last Supper).[13]

## *Jesus's Embodied Meaning:*
## *The Kingdom of God*

There are two historical facts about which all Jesus scholars agree: Jesus was crucified, and Jesus was baptized by John. This latter fact sets the stage for understanding the overarching set of expectations and excitement afoot in Jesus's Jewish world. Jesus followed John in his anticipation of eschatological judgment. There was a coming "day of wrath" in which God would judge Israel for its faithfulness or apostasy. Contrary to assumptions that this has to do with the end of the world, for Jesus and John and their contemporaries the focus was a climactic event that they

*[handwritten: theology concerned w/ death, judgment + final destiny of the soul + humankind]*

---

12 See Laughlin, *Jesus and the Cross,* 152–54. See also Mark D. Baker and Joel B. Green, *Recovering the Scandal of the Cross: Atonement in New Testament and Contemporary Contexts* (Downers Grove, IL: InterVarsity Press, 2011), 53–63.

13 In this section we rely heavily on Peter Laughlin's book, cited above, *Jesus and the Cross,* primarily chapter 4. He in turn relies on Ben F. Meyer, *The Aims of Jesus* (London: SCM Press, 1979); Wright, *Jesus and the Victory of God*; Scot McKnight, *Jesus and His Death: Historiography, the Historical Jesus, and Atonement Theory* (Waco: Baylor University Press, 2005); and James D. G. Dunn, *Jesus Remembered* (Grand Rapids, MI: Eerdmans, 2003).

*Is this why I don't worry about the end of the world/ 2nd coming? Because it is paired w/ mercy + reconciliation?*

expected to occur within the current space-time continuum.[14] Israel was the target of this preaching and many expected a great national disaster to be the harbinger of this divine judgment, perhaps at the mighty hands of Rome.

Still, if such divine judgment was well known in Jewish prophetic literature, so also was the theme of divine restoration. God's wrath was always in service of God's mercy and the cautionary warnings of eschatological judgment came with the expectation of renewal. A long line of prophetic witnesses proclaimed God's perpetual renewal of his covenant with Israel. In the world of Jesus and John, while Israel had been released from exile in Babylon, Israel as a nation was yet to be restored. The notion that God had yet to reconstitute his covenant with Israel and place her back in her rightful place on the world stage catalyzed great energy in Second Temple Judaism. For this hope, the phrase "kingdom of God" captured the imagination. As N. T. Wright puts it:

*So when Jesus speaks of the kingdom of God his listeners would envision a fully restored covenant not Heaven?*

We must stress, again, that this message [about the kingdom] is *part of a story*, and only makes sense as such. And there is only one story that will do. Israel would at last "return from exile"; evil would be defeated; YHWH would at last return to "visit" his people. Anyone wishing to evoke and affirm all this at once, in first-century Palestine, could not have chosen a more appropriate and ready-make slogan than "kingdom of god."[15]

*Is the implication of Heaven a theological projection of Gospel authors? In light of the resurrection?*

There is no doubt that Jesus appropriated this eschatological story as did John the Baptist and other Jews of his day. Jesus adapted the message to create his own unique proclamation. Among other things, Jesus's message shifted to focus more on the expected restoration and the signs of God's new acting rather than on God's imminent judgment. While a full discussion of how Jesus's mission differed from John's or from that of other first-century preachers would take us too far afield, we can note two themes.

---

14 Laughlin, *Jesus and the Cross,* 155. He here relies on N. T. Wright, *The New Testament and the People of God* (Minneapolis: Fortress Press, 1992), 208, 285–86, and Wright, *Jesus and The Victory of God,* 208–9.

15 Wright, *Jesus and the Victory of God,* 227. Note that the phrase "kingdom of God" as it appears in the New Testament refers not to a place but an action: the "ruling of God" or the "kingly rule of God."

First, Jesus declared that the new action of God was already partially realized. According to Mark, after John's arrest, Jesus began his ministry in Galilee, proclaiming, "The time is fulfilled, and the kingdom of God has come near; repent, and believe in the good news" (Mark 1:15). While *metanoia*—a complete reorientation of one's life—is required, Jesus's proclamation is one of good news since God is *already* acting in a new way.

Secondly, the shape of this new divine action, according to Jesus, was radically different from currently held convictions. He utterly subverted any nationalistic expectations. Rather than stress the political restoration of Israel, Jesus chose to emphasize Israel's role as a light to all nations. And Jesus himself embodied this new world by engaging with the poor, the unclean, and those entangled with demons. He healed and exorcised evil spirits, ate with the unwashed, and did not flinch from encounters with women of ill repute. Thus Jesus embraced the eschatological hope of his generation but wove into it meanings of liberation and healing that disrupted common expectations.[16]

Furthermore, while Jesus proclaims and embodies the reality of God's new work *now*, there is nevertheless a prospect of coming suffering prior to the full realization of God's kingdom. The new pattern that is life in the kingdom will not emerge without a period of great tribulation—the final ordeal. Strangely, evidence of this lies in the Lord's Prayer (Matt. 6:9–13 and Luke 11:2–4). The petition "Thy kingdom come" clearly sets the prayer in an eschatological light. But it is the sixth petition, to protect us from temptation—*peirasmos*—that warrants attention here. While this may refer to trials in general, many scholars read it as referring to the great tribulations that will precede the final entrance of the kingdom

---

16 Christopher Bryan puts it thus: "From Judas the Galilean to Simon Bar-Kokhba, all we know of them tells us that they taught that Israel's purity and faithfulness *must be preserved from the pagan invader by violence if necessary.* Jesus, however, taught a way to the Kingdom that came through peace, love, and a cross. The kinds of sayings collected in the Sermon on the Mount make clear that to fight the battles of the Kingdom with the enemy's weapons would mean that in fact the enemy had already won. The Roman soldier who commands the Galilean peasant to carry his baggage is therefore to be met with courtesy and generosity (Matt. 5:41). Those who are enemies of the state are not necessarily God's enemies, and if Israel is really the child of her heavenly father she will love them and pray for them (5:43–48)" (private e-mail correspondence, April 6, 2015; emphasis in original).

into history.[17] This will be the great testing of faith whereby evil itself is manifested to challenge the saints and weed out false prophets and saviors. While it will result in the ultimate victory of God over the evil one, it will confront the faithful with the great danger of apostasy. No wonder Jesus exhorts his followers to pray that they be spared this time of temptation and rescued from (the) evil (one).

Not only can we assume that Jesus exhorted his followers to ask for help in the face of this coming ordeal, it seems that Jesus anticipated this final ordeal for his own life. In the garden of Gethsemane Jesus warns his disciples to stay awake so that they might avoid the *peirasmos* (Mark 14:38). Jesus's own petitions to be spared his impending punishment and death reflect the sixth petition of the Lord's Prayer. If Jesus saw his mission and ministry as the beginning of the new work of God, he also understood that this new work would be initiated by eschatological tribulation. And he seemed to see his own suffering and death as part and parcel of the introduction of the new age. In some way Jesus's ordeal would be the catalyst for God's great victory.[18]

Hence, while we do not have access to Jesus's inner thought processes, there is enough evidence in what the disciples recalled and recorded, in light of what we know about Jesus's era, to say a number of things. Jesus certainly lived and preached eschatological hope in the new way that God was acting in Israel, in both judging and renewing God's covenant with Israel in history. This hope lay in transforming Israel, not into a restored political entity, but into a renewed community that would function as a light to all nations. The transformed life of the kingdom was already partially enacted in Jesus's own life, as evidenced in his healings, exorcisms, and encounters with people on the margins or in everyday life. His embodied kingdom life went against the grain of many common Jewish expectations. It also incorporated a narrative in which the final victory of God over evil forces would be accomplished, but not without great tribulations, tribulations that holy persons would experience as a testing of their faith. Jesus saw his own suffering and death

---

17 See McKnight, *Jesus and His Death,* 106–15, and Meyer, *Aims of Jesus,* 206–8; Much earlier both Joachim Jeremias and Raymond Brown took this approach to the Lord's Prayer. See Joachim Jeremias, *The Prayers of Jesus* (London: SCM, 1967), 105–6, and Raymond E. Brown, "The Pater Noster as an Eschatological Prayer," in *New Testament Essays* (New York: Image Books, 1968), 314–16.

18 See Meyer, *Aims of Jesus,* 216.

foreshadowed in that of John and the earlier prophets. In anticipating his death, he also anticipated that he and his faithful followers would be vindicated in the end.[19]

## Jesus's Spoken Meaning: What Did He Say about His Death?

Jesus clearly anticipated his own death. He portrayed himself as the one rejected by the Jewish authorities of his day, as the prophets had been rejected of old.[20] He spoke openly about his expected suffering, rejection, and death.[21] It is noteworthy, however, that he said very little about *Hmmm* just what he thought his death would mean. His death and its aftermath was not the focal point of his teaching; the new reign of God was. In particular, Jesus did not explicitly ascribe *salvific* meaning to his death *WOW* per se.

There are three sets of passages in which Jesus spoke about his death and its potential meaning. These include the passion predictions,[22] the ransom saying of Mark 10:45 (= Matt.20:28), and the words instituting the Lord's Supper. The passion predictions are variations—with more or less expansion—of the following: the Son of Man is to undergo great suffering, be rejected by the (Jewish) powers-that-be, be killed, and after three days rise again. The hand of the Gospel authors is apparent here, most obviously in Mark, where he places each of the three predictions in chapters 8, 9, and 10 just before some incident in which the disciples clearly misunderstand the nature of their journey to Jerusalem. Among other things Mark was telling his followers that being a disciple of Jesus was not all sweetness and light but meant embracing the suffering that faithfulness to Jesus would entail. In spite of this obvious editorial interpretation, a few points about Jesus's intentions are warranted.

---

19 See Laughlin, *Jesus and the Cross,* 163–78, Meyer, *Aims of Jesus,* 216–17, and Wright, *Jesus and the Victory of God,* 336–39. For an alternative view that puts less emphasis on the eschatological focus of Jesus's ministry, see Stephen Finlan, *Problems with Atonement* (Collegeville, MN: Liturgical Press, 2005), 111–13 and Stephen Finlan, *Options on Atonement in Christian Thought* (Collegeville, MN: Liturgical Press, 2007), 35–36.

20 See, for example, the parable of the vineyard in Mark 12:1–9 and the condemnation of "this generation" in Luke 11:47–51.

21 See McKnight, *Jesus and His Death,* 79–81, wherein Laughlin counts 37 relevant passages (Laughlin, *Jesus and the Cross,* 166n62).

22 Mark 8:31, 9:31, 10:33–34, and parallels in Matt. 16:13–23 and Luke 9:18–22.

An important but often overlooked element is Jesus's use of the term "Son of Man." Interestingly, this appellation appears in the New Testament only on the lips of Jesus, in reference to himself. He is never referred to as Son of Man by anyone else, nor does this become a term of worship in the early church.[23] This is a hint that "Son of Man" is a key to understanding Jesus's view of himself. While the term can refer merely to "a human being," given the eschatological vision of Jesus's entire mission, it is more likely to be a reference to the book of Daniel, chapter 7.[24] This book fits in the category of apocalyptic literature, like the book of Revelation in the New Testament. It is full of visions and imagery, written two centuries before Jesus in light of the persecution of the Jews by the Syrian-Greek ruler Antiochus IV Epiphanes. In a vision recorded in Daniel 7, Daniel sees "one like a son of man" coming on the clouds of heaven. This son of man is presented to the Ancient One (God) and given dominion over all peoples and nations (vv. 13–14). This is a scene of vindication to follow the era when the holy ones of the Most High (those faithful to YHWH) will be given over to the power of "the beast" for a period of time (v. 25).

It seems that Jesus took over these images—both of the holy ones subjected to evil powers and of the one who would come as the harbinger of their vindication—and applied them to himself. While the formulated words of the passion predictions show the hand of those who knew the outcome of events, they still convey that Jesus in some way foresaw his rejection by the religious authorities of his day, anticipated his death, and yet saw in these expected events the action of God. If indeed Jesus took upon himself the designation "Son of Man" with all the connotations of God's new ruling power in the world, he saw his death as fulfilling both the burden of God's abandonment of Israel (his "wrath") as well as its vindication.[25]

In addition to the passion predictions, the saying about "ransom" in

23 See Dunn, *Jesus Remembered,* 737. He notes the one exception in Acts 7:56 when Stephen is being stoned and proclaims that he sees the Son of Man standing at the right hand of God, reflecting Jesus's words in Luke 22:69.

24 See Wright, *Jesus and the Victory of God,* 512–16.

25 The many interpretations of the various "son of man" sayings of Jesus is vast and confusing. Wright makes a case for the historicity of Jesus's use of the phrase in his own creative way, in an eschatological framework. See Wright, *Jesus and the Victory of God,* 512–16. For a detailed examination of the importance of the Son of Man in reference to Jesus's understanding of his own death, see Laughlin, *Jesus and the Cross,* 170–78.

Mark 10:45 (= Matt. 20:28) provides another place where Jesus spoke explicitly about his death and its meaning. "For the Son of Man came not to be served but to serve, and to give his life a ransom for many." The idea that Jesus's death served as a ransom paid to free sinners from bondage would become a prime metaphor for theologies of salvation in centuries to come. As will be discussed in the next chapter, the ransom imagery led to questions about to whom the ransom was paid—God? The devil? None of that is in this passage. Jesus says nothing about what he pays in his death nor to whom. There is no reference to a transaction here.[26]

*Good ques* [handwritten margin note]

Rather, the passage needs to be put in its narrative and historical context. The verse comes just after one of those major misunderstandings following a passion prediction (Mark 10:33–34). James and John come forward and ask for special privileges once Jesus comes into his glory (vv. 35–37). The other disciples are enraged and jealousy rules the day. Jesus gathers them together and says that, unlike the power mongering that goes on in their current culture, they are to submit to one another. "Whoever wishes to become great among you must be your servant, and whoever wishes to be first among you must be slave of all" (vv. 43–44). And then the climax: "For the Son of Man came not to be served but to serve, and to give his life a ransom for many." (v. 45)

Historically, the world of patronage that dominated the Roman world of Jesus's day cannot be overstated. Everyone had a place in society, a role that included those to whom one paid homage and those from whom one expected homage. Sons had duties to fathers, slaves to their masters, clients to their patrons, and lower-class clients to those with upper-class connections. Those in positions of patronage were likewise obligated to care for the poor and the weak.[27] All were ultimately indebted to the Emperor, who himself owed allegiance to the gods. This system found its primordial foundation in the rule of the gods: it was sacred.[28] The

---

26 See Laughlin, *Jesus and the Cross,* 178–79. Because this attribution of ransom to Jesus's death is so singular—appearing only here in Mark and its parallel in Matthew—it is understood by some to be the reflection of Mark or his community, imputed back to a saying of Jesus about servanthood. For a defense of this ransom saying as authentically that of Jesus, see references in Baker and Green, *Recovering the Scandal,* 55n9. For a complete dismissal of Jesus as its source, see Finlan, *Options on Atonement,* 37.

*theo projection of author* [handwritten margin note]

27 See, for example, the parables of the Rich Fool (Luke 12:16–20) and Dives and Lazarus (Luke 16:19–31) in which the failure of patrons in their duties is at stake.

28 See Baker and Green, *Recovering the Scandal,* 56.

followers of Judaism in the first century depended for their survival (literally and figuratively) on holding their own within this hierarchical system.

Against this, Jesus's message presses against the grain. He preached—in word and action—a kingdom that belonged to little children, in which sinners and the unclean would be welcome. The kingdom would involve a community that started small—like a mustard seed—and would be measured by one's role as a servant. The plea of James and John, as well as debates about greatness among the disciples in general (Mark 9:33–34), reveal the disciples' capitulation to a culture of patronage. Jesus' words overturning this were remembered in many forms, not least of which was this reversal whereby the leader of the community becomes its servant. That the Son of Man "gives his life as a ransom for many" merely but significantly indicates that the person who will vindicate Israel (Jesus) will do so through overturning power expectations, to the point of death.

"Ransom" is the Greek word *lytron,* which means "means of release" or "deliverance." To understand its meaning in this context, we can point to two sources. The first is the slave trade in the ancient world.[29] As practiced in the first century, a price could be paid to free a slave, at which point that slave would belong to the one who paid for his or her emancipation. Perhaps more significant is the use of the word in the Greek translation of the Hebrew scriptures in which the word *lytron* is used to describe God's freeing of Israel from bondage in Egypt: "I am the Lord, and I will free you from the burdens of the Egyptians and deliver you from slavery to them. I will redeem [*lytron*] you with an outstretched arm and with mighty acts of judgment" (Exod. 6:6). In this light, Jesus's giving of his life is part of the narrative of a new exodus, a new liberation of Israel from bondage.

## Jesus's Symbolic Meaning:
### The Temple and the Last Supper

Historical scholarship agrees that, in addition to words, Jesus used symbolic actions to convey the meaning of his mission. This is particularly true in the two symbolic deeds that stand as bookends to the last week

---

29 See http://www.ancient.eu/article/629/. Accessed Jan. 17, 2016.

of Jesus's life: his provocative disruption in the temple and his actions at the Last Supper. That the two events are inextricably linked is accepted by most scholars; just what they mean is a further question.

Just what happened when Jesus cleansed the temple? And what meanings did Jesus expect to invoke in this incident?[30] Jesus upsets the tables of the moneychangers and dove sellers, and restricts movement through the temple. It is a misnomer to call this a "cleansing" of the temple, since it was in no way a ritual act of purification—something only the priests could do. Likewise, it does not seem that Jesus is condemning the practice of providing the animals needed for sacrifices in the temple. People would make long journeys from great distances to bring their offerings, and transporting birds or lambs all the way from Egypt or Italy was impractical.[31] The buying and selling constituted a set of support services for the important work of the temple rituals.

It is unlikely, then, that Jesus was merely critiquing corruption in the way that this merchandising was taking place. His critique went deeper. Isaiah, Ezekiel, and Jeremiah had all undertaken dramatic actions in their day to illustrate the apostasy of Israel and the coming judgment of God as a result.[32] As a prophet in his own right, Jesus undertakes dramatic action to symbolize that something had gone dramatically wrong with the existing temple.[33] What did he think this was? Given his eschatological focus as well as his reinterpretation of the coming restoration of Israel, we can see in this "cleansing" that Jesus is subverting not temple practices per se, but the entitlement and nationalism embedded in them. "Far from becoming a light to the nations Israel had become myopic,

---

30 The incident is recorded in all four gospels, though its placement in John is at the beginning of Jesus's ministry as a symbolic gesture foreshadowing his death and resurrection. In the synoptic Gospels the temple disturbance comes at the end of Jesus's life and, most explicitly in Mark, serves as the reason he is arrested. See Mark 11:15–18, Matthew 21:12–13, Luke 19:45–46, John 2:13–16.

31 See Laughlin, *Jesus and the Cross,* 189. He refers to Paula Fredriksen, *Jesus of Nazareth, King of the Jews: A Jewish Life and the Emergence of Christianity* (London: Macmillan, 1999), 209. Note that Jesus's parents made such a journey to offer a sacrifice of thanksgiving after his birth: Luke 2:22–24. They would have needed to buy "a pair of turtle-doves or two young pigeons" (v. 24) in order to do this.

32 See Isaiah 20:1–6 (nakedness), Ezekiel 4:1–7 (brick), Jeremiah 19:1–15 (smashed pot). Discussed in Laughlin, *Jesus and the Cross,* 190.

33 He was not alone in this judgment given evidence that both the Qumram and Essene communities likewise criticized the existing Temple. See Laughlin, *Jesus and the Cross,* 190n133.

unable to see past its own nationalistic ideals."[34] His reference to Isaiah's insistence that the temple be a "house of prayer for all peoples" combined with Jeremiah's complaint about a "den of robbers," supports this interpretation.[35] His overturning of the tables is thus a symbolic gesture that prefigures the coming judgment of God upon Israel.[36]

Jesus further hints at a new temple to come. He prophesizes the destruction of the temple (Mark 13:2) and indicates that this will instigate the building of a temple "not made with hands" (Mark 14:58, John 2:19). Jesus himself is the key to the inauguration of this reconstituted temple in the new age of God's kingdom. More specifically, it seems that Jesus's death will instigate the installation of this new covenantal symbol and community. That this is the case leads us to the symbolic meaning of the Last Supper.

The institution of what came to be known as the Lord's Supper, or the Eucharist, appears in three Gospels and Paul's first letter to the Corinthians (Mark 14:22–25; Matt. 26:26–29; Luke 22:14–23; 1 Cor. 11:23–26).[37] Paul's is the earliest of these accounts. Also interesting is that his account of the Eucharist is embedded in his chastisement of his followers for the discord, divisions, and inhospitability that was rife among them. The Gospel of Luke likewise situates the Last Supper just prior to debates among the disciples as to which one of them is greatest (Luke 22:24–27). A shared meal in the ancient world created solidarity amongst participants. The symbolic meaning that Jesus constituted at the Last Supper was in line with this expectation of unity while challenging any hierarchy of importance amongst his disciples.[38]

What then can we say about the meanings that Jesus himself sought to enact by appealing to his body and blood? That eating bread and drinking wine became the core of Christian worship early on is well attested. Indeed, Paul introduces his account by saying "For I received

---

34 Laughlin, *Jesus and the Cross,* 191.

35 See Isaiah 56:7 and Jerermiah 7:11.

36 For another view, see Finlan, *Problems with Atonement,* 113.

37 Although there is a "last supper" scene in John, it does not involve the institution of the Eucharist. Rather, this is the occasion of the washing of the disciples' feet, which many traditions today celebrate on Holy Thursday. However, in John 6:51–58 Jesus declares himself to be the living bread come from heaven and refers to those who "eat my flesh and drink my blood" as having eternal life.

38 See Baker and Green, *Recovering the Scandal,* 59–60.

from the Lord what I also handed on to you," indicating that there was already an established tradition of eucharistic practice leading back to Jesus himself. Likewise it is evident that the early Christians interpreted Jesus's death in sacrificial terms. First Corinthians 5:7 says, "Our paschal lamb, Christ, has been sacrificed." Hebrews 10:1–18 elaborates on Christ as the final sacrifice for sins. While symbolic actions can always convey multiple meanings, we need to delve a bit deeper to get at what the event and Jesus's appeal to bread and wine would have meant for Jesus.

The first issue to note has to do with exactly when this meal took place. The Gospel of John places it on the night before Passover, so that Jesus is crucified on Passover. The synoptic Gospels treat it as a Passover meal, taking place on Passover itself. Scholarly opinion has sided with the former chronology, placing the meal on the night prior to Passover.[39] It is notable that Jesus did not symbolize his anticipated death in terms of the paschal lamb, using bread and wine instead. So while his meaning was clearly embedded in the Passover context as a whole, he did not explicitly see himself as the sacrificial lamb. Instead, the reference to bread likely referred to the "bread of affliction," meaning the suffering of the Israelites in Egypt symbolized at Passover by unleavened bread. Jesus offers this bread—his broken body—as his bearing of the affliction of Israel in the final ordeal. His followers are to accept this gift by eating this symbol of his willingness to suffer the coming judgment of Israel on its behalf. He creates new meaning out of the Exodus tradition in light of the coming kingdom and his anticipated death.

This Exodus narrative can further apply to Jesus's blood. All four passages refer to Jesus's blood as the "cup of the new covenant." This reference to covenant is unique in Jesus's mission; he has not used this language heretofore, preferring the image of the kingdom. While this leads some scholars to suggest that the covenant language is a later addition, given Jesus's eschatological emphasis on what God is doing anew, the meaning can still stand whether Jesus used the word "covenant" or not.[40] The referent here is the solidification of the covenant between Israel and YHWH after the Exodus, as recounted in Exodus 24:8. At Mt. Sinai, the people pledge to follow the laws YHWH has provided, and

---

39 See Raymond E. Brown, *The Death of the Messiah: From Gethsemane to the Grave*, vol. 1 (New York: Doubleday, 1994), 1350–76, esp. 1371–73.

40 For comparison, see Finlan, *Problems with Atonement*, 114, and Finlan, *Options on Atonement in Christian Thought*, 38–40.

Moses sprinkles them with blood saying, "See the blood of the covenant that the LORD has made with you in accordance with all these words." This is not the same as the blood of the lamb that protected people from the plague of death in Egypt. But the two uses of blood are part of the same narrative, of God protecting Israel from harsh judgment, liberating her from bondage, and establishing a covenant with her.

Laughlin concludes his review of the literature as follows:

> Therefore what Jesus is doing in the Last Supper is drawing upon the stories of the Passover, exodus and covenant and stunningly connecting them to his own body and blood, that is, his own death. . . . Jesus intended to claim that the new exodus, the return of YHWH the king, would ultimately come about through his own death. It is thus the symbolism of the Last Supper that dramatically connects Jesus' expectation of suffering and death with the eschatological coming of the kingdom.[41]

Laughlin goes on to add a caution:

> However, as always, we must be careful to avoid reading later theological understandings back into Jesus' constituted meaning. What has been outlined here is perhaps the minimal that can be said; Jesus created the symbolism of the Last Supper to reveal that God's eschatological work (occurring in and through him) would redeem his followers for life within the new covenant community and to guarantee them a place at the eschatological banquet to come.[42]

In conclusion, what can we say about the meaning that Jesus himself constituted for his ministry and anticipated death? While we must infer these meanings from the impact that they had on his followers, contextual historical research supports the following. Jesus saw himself as a prophet in line with the Hebrew prophets of old as well as with John's more recent mission. He proclaimed an eschatological kingdom—that God was doing something new in the world. This new action of God

41 Laughlin, *Jesus and the Cross,* 204.
42 Ibid., 205.

would come with judgment and tribulation for Israel, prior to its restoration. This restoration, contrary to expectations at the time, would bring Israel back to its calling as a light to all nations and would draw in the marginalized and the "least" of society.

Jesus knew that his message was extremely countercultural. He anticipated his rejection by the powerful of his day. In expecting his rejection and death, he saw himself as enduring the final ordeal—the wrath of God—on behalf of those loyal to the kingdom, his followers. Yet this ordeal would be the catalyst for a new way of being in the world, under God's rule. He symbolized this dramatically by his disruption in the temple and by constituting bread and wine as symbols of his death, initiating a new exodus from bondage into a reconstituted covenant community.

This is a minimal theology of transformation and is a long way from the theologies of salvation that would develop in subsequent decades and centuries, post-Easter. To see how this theological enlargement begins to unfold, we turn to the theology that Paul creates in light of his own experience of the risen Lord and his mission to the Gentiles.

# Paul

While Paul is the earliest New Testament example we have of struggling with the meaning of Jesus's death in light of the resurrection, it appears that there already existed a kind of creedal tradition before Paul began writing. In 1 Corinthians 15 he indicates this when he says, "For I handed on to you as of first importance what I in turn had received: that Christ *died for our sins* in accordance with the scriptures, and that he was buried, and that he was raised on the third day in accordance with the scriptures, and that he appeared to Cephas, then to the twelve" (vv. 3–5, emphasis added).[43] His opening salutation to the Galatians offers

---

43 There are several things to note about this passage. First, "in accordance with the scriptures" clearly refers to the Law and the Prophets, that is, the Jewish scriptures, since Christian "scriptures" would not exist for several centuries. Second, Paul records the appearance of the risen Lord to Cephas and the twelve and over five hundred brothers and sisters (vv. 3–6). Curiously, he does not mention the empty tomb or the women who discovered it. Either he simply had not inherited this tradition, or he chose to highlight the appearances since he himself will—just a few verses later—include himself in the list of those who witnessed a postresurrection encounter with Jesus (v. 8).

grace and peace from God "and the Lord Jesus Christ, *who gave himself for our sins* to set us free from the present evil age" (1:3–4, emphasis added).[44] Paul was a masterfully creative and passionate theologian who took an existing tradition—he was, after all, a bit late to the faith—and developed it for his own purposes.

Volumes could be (and have been) written in an attempt to get to the heart of Paul's "gospel." Our limited scope here can touch only on some important points. The main task is to show that even though Paul uses language about blood and sacrifice and salvation from God's wrath, he does not in any way endorse a view of atonement that implies God as vengeful or violent, or that envisions Jesus's crucifixion as a punishment he received in our stead. The key points we want to unfold with regard to Paul's theology include the following:

1. Whatever the atonement achieved, it was in order that we might live new lives in Christ. Christ's work was for *us*, not because *God* needed something in order to accept or love us.

2. Christ's death is part of God's action in reconciling us to Godself but not as a substitution for our death. The key point in the *sacrifice* that Christ made is his obedience and willingness to abide in God in spite of oppressive evil powers aligned against him, at the price of his life.

3. The resurrection (Christ's as well as our own) is as much a part of the reconciliation achieved in the Christ event as is the crucifixion.

4. For Paul, the center of the gospel is our *participation* in the new life of the risen Lord. This participation involves us as well in sharing in his death, which is an embrace of our own death to the sin that enslaves us and a willingness to suffer the consequences of living faithful lives in Christ.

---

44 In addition, in his earliest letter, to the Thessalonians, Paul's greeting incorporates his pride in them in that they "turned to God from idols, to serve the living and true God, and to wait for his Son from heaven, *whom he raised from the dead—Jesus, who rescues us from the wrath that is coming*" (1 Thess.1:9b–10, emphasis added). This latter phrase can indicate a pre-Pauline basic creedal affirmation, as well as a reference to Jewish apocalyptic expectations (the "wrath to come"). For comments on this and other potential pre-Pauline elements in Paul's letters, see Gerard S. Sloyan, *The Crucifixion of Jesus: History, Myth, Faith* (Minneapolis: Fortress Press, 1995), 47, 65.

To begin, let us examine two important concepts that Paul takes up from his Jewish heritage. They are two sides of the same concern: the *justice of God* and the *wrath of God*.[45]

## The Justice of God and the Wrath of God

Paul is insistent that the human condition is fraught with sin and oppression. He takes this for granted but presses the point that *all* have sinned and fallen short of the glory of God. He hammers home this point in the early chapters of Romans, emphasizing that Jews have no advantage over Gentiles, nor do the Gentiles have an excuse because they did not receive the Law. Paul is harsh in his judgment of humans and their sinfulness on all sides.

However, we import to his world a modern way of thinking if we imagine God's justice as some kind of balance sheet or legal ledger. Our modern notions of justice emphasize impartiality in the sense of disengagement and neutrality on the part of judge or jury. Both the Jewish and the Pauline notions of God's justice are quite different, mainly because they begin with *relationship*. We cannot understand God apart from the covenant God has made with humankind, specifically with the people of Israel. God's justice is about *restoring* that covenant relationship when it is broken. Hence, God's justice can never be understood without a grasp of God's mercy and love.

The Hebrew word for "justice" in the Old Testament (*tsedaqah*), while at times retaining a legal sense, as often refers to God's saving actions. "I [God] bring near my deliverance (*tsedaqah*), it is not far off, and my salvation will not tarry" (Isa. 46:13). "In his days Judah will be saved and Israel will live in safety. And this is the name by which he will be called: 'the LORD is our righteousness'" (Jer. 23: 6). "I [the psalmist] have not hidden your saving help (*tsedaqah*) within my heart, I have spoken of your faithfulness and your salvation" (Psa. 40:10). God is harsh when it comes to those who take "the day of the Lord" for granted

---

45 I rely in this section on Anthony J. Tambasco, *A Theology of Atonement and Paul's Vision of Christianity* (Collegeville MN: Liturgical Press, 1991). See also Baker and Green, *Recovering the Scandal*, esp. chapters 2–4.

(Amos).[46] He does punish those who betray their covenant commitments through idolatry or hypocrisy, though even in these cases it is more that God allows sin to reap its own consequences than that God imposes a penalty. God certainly never acts as a neutral arbiter. Rather God's justice and God's mercy/saving action always go hand in hand. Furthermore, the deliverance brought by God's justice is a communal one. The entire community is brought right through God's saving actions; it is not merely a case of individual salvation.[47]

Paul brings this full-bodied notion of God's *saving* justice into his interpretation of Christ's work. God's justice as deliverance is now newly manifest in Christ—Christ crucified and risen, a stumbling block to Jews and foolishness to Greeks (1 Cor. 1). God, who has chosen what is foolish in the world (a crucified savior), has made Christ the source of justice and salvation: "He [God] is the source of your life in Christ Jesus, who became for us wisdom from God, and righteousness and sanctification and redemption" (1 Cor. 1:30).

In the letter to the Romans, Paul takes on the corollary question: if God had already offered deliverance through the Law, what is new in Christ, or why would God manifest God's justice/deliverance in a new way? Paul's answer is twofold: (1) because the Law does not deliver us from sin but makes us aware of sin and heightens sin's proclivity and (2) so that God's salvation could be offered to all, Gentiles as well as Jews.

A few key passages indicate this:

> For I am not ashamed of the gospel; it is the power of God for salvation to everyone who has faith, to the Jew first and also to the Greek. For in it the righteousness of God is revealed through faith for faith; as it is written, "The one who is righteous will live by faith." (Rom. 1:16–17)

> But now, irrespective of law, the righteousness of God has been disclosed, and is attested by the law and the prophets, the righteousness of God through faith in Jesus Christ for all who believe. For there is no distinction,

---

46 See Amos 5:18ff. Apparently some in Israel were counting on the day of the Lord as a time when other nations would be judged and Israel vindicated. God indicates that they, too, will come under judgment for their hypocrisy.

47 The entire corpus of prophetic writings attests to this, but Second Isaiah—Isaiah 40–55—serves as a good example.

since all have sinned and fall short of the glory of God; they are now justified by his grace as a gift, through the redemption that is in Christ Jesus, whom God put forward as a sacrifice of atonement by his blood, effective through faith. He did this to show his righteousness, because in his divine forbearance he had passed over the sins previously committed; it was to prove at the present time that he himself is righteous and that he justifies the one who has faith in Jesus. (Rom. 3:21–26)[48]

So if God's justice is his activity to save, what do we make of God's wrath? The notion that gods are to be feared, especially because of their potential anger, may have primitive roots, even within the Jewish scriptures (for example, see Exod. 32:7–10). Most scholars, however, acknowledge that this Old Testament notion evolves to the point where "wrath" is more about an activity of God in response to sin than merely an irrational anger on God's part.[49] God's wrath is indeed a *pathos*—a passionate response to sin—but it is a fully rational passion; a "NO" in the face of the evil that humans perpetuate generation after generation. As C. E. B. Cranfield says:

> We shall not understand what Paul means by the wrath of God, until we recognize, first, that, in seeking the measure of help which human analogies can afford, we must look not to the lower, irrational kind of human anger, but to the higher kind, the indignation against injustice, cruelty and corruption, which is an essential element of goodness and love in a world in which moral evil is present; and, secondly, that even the very highest and purest human wrath can at the best afford but a distorted and twisted reflection of the wrath of

---

48 E. P. Sanders notes that "righteousness" as a noun has no easy verbal equivalent in English, so "justifies" is usually used. This imports a legal connotation (reflected by Luther and passed on to the modern era) that is not quite right with regard to Paul. Sanders suggests the phrase "to righteous" as an alternative. With this suggestion, the last line of this quote would read "that he righteouses the one who has faith in Jesus." The point is that this is not about an external ledger but about a change within the believer. See Sanders, *Paul*, 53–58. For Sanders comments on Luther's (mistaken) understanding of this, see ibid, 57–58.

49 For more on God's wrath, see Tambasco, *Theology of Atonement*, 31–34, and Baker and Green, *Recovering the Scandal*, 70–77.

> God, since the wrath of men (our Lord alone excepted) is always more or less compromised by the presence of sin in the one who is wroth, whereas the wrath of God is the wrath of Him who is perfectly loving, perfectly good.[50]

Thus God's wrath in the first-century context is both a passionate contradiction of human evil and an objective force that will issue in consequences for those who turn from God. In particular, it is associated with a future event when God will cleanse the earth of sin. This is the "day of the Lord." Zephaniah says, "The great day of the LORD is near, near and hastening fast. . . . That day will be a day of wrath, a day of distress and anguish, a day of ruin and devastation, a day of darkness and gloom, a day of clouds and thick darkness" (Zeph. 1:14–15). So the "wrath to come" and the "day of wrath" as used by Paul would have been clear allusions to the apocalyptic expectations of his day. He refers to "Jesus, who rescues us from the wrath that is to come" (1 Thess. 1:10).

The most extensive discussion of God's judgment in Paul comes in Romans, chapter 1:18–31. He is setting up his argument for the salvation of all (Jew and Gentile) by indicating that God's righteousness brooks no compromise with those who fail to acknowledge God as God. "For the wrath of God is revealed from heaven against all ungodliness and wickedness of those who by their wickedness suppress the truth" (v. 18). Neither Jew nor Gentile has any excuse since God has made himself plain to all. Note here that God's judgment is not against specific persons or actions. Rather the offense is an entire attitude and disposition (that of idolatry, of substituting worship of creatures for worship of the true God). Note, further, that the sins listed here such as lust, gossip, envy, rebelliousness toward parents, and same-sex relations, are the *evidence* of God's wrath, not the *cause* of it. Three times in this passage (vv. 24, 26, 28) Paul says that "God gave them up"—to lusts, passions, a debased mind. In other words, God's wrath is *already apparent* in God's abandonment of these sinners to their own destiny. God's wrath has to do with allowing sin to work its own destruction.

It is this situation, in which all have sinned and suffered the wrath of God by experiencing the dead end of sinful lives, to which Christ's

---

50 C. E. B. Cranfield, *The Epistle to the Romans*, 2 vols., The International Critical Commentary (Edinburgh: T & T Clark, 1975–79), I:108.

salvation speaks. So we get to Romans 3, the apex of Paul's argument at the beginning of Romans: *"But now,* irrespective of law, the righteousness of God has been disclosed, and is attested by the law and the prophets, the righteousness of God through faith in Jesus Christ for all who believe" (vv. 21–22, emphasis added). "They are now justified by his grace as a gift, through the redemption that is in Christ Jesus, whom God put forward as a sacrifice of atonement by his blood, effective through faith" (24–25a).

So God's wrath is manifested in God's allowing sin to run its full course, but this is in service of God's saving activity (God's justice). God has "endured with much patience the objects of wrath that are made for destruction . . . in order to make known the riches of his glory for the objects of mercy—including us whom he has called, not from the Jews only but from the Gentiles" (Rom. 9:22–24). So while Paul does not mince words when it comes to the fruits of sin and God's displeasure with it, his objective is to drive home the "but now" of salvation. For "God has destined us not for wrath but for obtaining salvation through our Lord Jesus Christ" (1 Thess. 5:9). God's wrath and God's justice are two sides of the same coin. Both have a future dimension in the closure that will come with the apocalyptic return of the Lord. But Paul's overriding concern is the present *new* reality that is manifested in the community of Christ's followers, both Jew and Gentile alike.

## Christ as Sacrifice

Nevertheless, the Romans 3 quotation above makes very apparent that a *sacrifice of atonement* is part of the equation when it comes to this new thing God is doing in Christ. What are we to make of the sacrificial imagery in Paul's letters?

It seems clear that Paul inherited a tradition that connected Jesus's death to liberation from sin. So the notion that "Christ died for our sins" (1 Cor. 15: 3) and that he "gave himself for our sins" (Gal. 1:4) was received by Paul and developed for his own pastoral purposes. So, we find passages such as:

> For while we were still weak, at the right time Christ
> died for the ungodly. Indeed, rarely will anyone die for a
> righteous person—though perhaps for a good person one

might actually dare to die. But God proves his love for us in that while we still were sinners Christ died for us. (Rom. 5:6–8)

For God destined us not for wrath but for obtaining salvation through our Lord Jesus Christ, who died for us, so that whether we are awake or asleep [live or die] we may live for him. (1 Thess. 5:9–10)

For the love of Christ urges us on, because we are convinced that one has died for all; therefore all have died. And he died for all, so that those who live might live no longer for themselves, but for him who died and was raised for them. (2 Cor. 5:14–15)

The question arises as to how it was that Christ's death was so quickly and directly connected to freeing humankind from sin. Paul himself was not the least bit interested in the historical details of Christ's crucifixion. He was more interested in the present effect that it had on converts' lives. And he clearly associated the death and resurrection with freeing *all*—Jews and Gentiles—from the burden of sin.

Some scholars have suggested that the background to this atoning death lies in the "noble martyr" tradition that had developed from the time of the Maccabees, most evident in 4 Maccabees.[51] Others insist that the early Christians found an interpretive tool in the image of the "Suffering Servant" of Isaiah 53, though this was not part of Jewish expectations nor is it directly quoted in the New Testament.[52] Most scholars, however, while acknowledging these as potential cultural background images, insist that the temple cultic practices would have been a more direct connection. As Gerard Sloyan puts it,

The whole of temple sacrifice was geared to liberating the people from the effects of sin. For that reason it should not surprise us that when an innocent man was viewed as yielding up his life freely he should have been seen as an offering for sin. . . . The whole Jewish

---

51 See Sloyan, *Crucifixion of Jesus,* 57ff.
52 See Tambasco, *Theology of Atonement,* 66–68.

culture was familiar with animal victims symbolic of the repentant human spirit. It was a short step from there to seeing in this sinless human victim Jesus an expiatory sin offering.[53]

The passage that most clearly makes this connection is Romans 3:23–25a:

> Since all have sinned and fall short of the glory of God; they are now justified by his grace as a gift, through the redemption that is in Christ Jesus, whom God put forward as a sacrifice of atonement [*hilasterion* in Greek] by his blood, effective through faith.

Whether or not this passage predates Paul or is his original language, it seems clear that temple sacrifice sets the framework in which Christ's death was seen as atoning for sins. The problem that arises is in understanding correctly the meaning and practice of temple sacrifices in the first place. While a complete examination of temple practices is not possible here, several points need to be made.[54]

First, "sacrifices" and "offerings" were the same thing, and were, in general, a way of solidifying one's relationship with God. They were undertaken as acts of thanksgiving or regular acts of worship. Some sacrifices were indeed undertaken as sin offerings or guilt offerings, but even in these cases the focus was on purity in relation to "holy things" more than on moral misbehavior. So, for example, a sin offering would be offered for a woman after childbirth or a leper who was healed as a way of "cleansing" them after impurity.[55]

Second, while some rituals did involve killing animals (which kinds of animal depended on how wealthy you were, for the most part), the purifying element was not the death of the animal per se. Rather, the

---

53 Sloyan, *Crucifixion of Jesus*, 69.

54 Leviticus 1–7 is the most direct Old Testament reference for the five kinds of sacrifices that were made for and by the priests of the temple. For more on this, see http://www.studylight.org/dic/hbd/view.cgi?number=T5431 and http://www.biblestudytools.com/dictionaries/bakers-evangelical-dictionary/offerings-and-sacrifices.html. Accessed May 25, 2015.

55 This is illustrated in the New Testament by the story of Jesus telling the leper to go offer "the gift that Moses commanded" after healing him. See Matthew 8:1–4 (Mark 1:40–45; Luke 5:12–16). Mary's purification after childbirth could be part of the rationale for the sacrifice that Mary and Joseph make at the temple in Luke 2:22–24.

focus was on the blood, which symbolized life, not death, and was sprinkled around the altar as a way for the repentant person to offer his life back to God. The key here is Leviticus 17:11: "For the life of the flesh is in the blood; and I have given it to you for making atonement for your lives on the altar; for, as life, it is the blood that makes atonement." Indeed, the penitent lays his hands on the animal before it dies so that his sins are transferred.[56] But what is offered to God is not the *death* of the animal but its *life,* represented by its blood, symbolizing the sinner's release from sin to be reunited with God.[57]

Third, in technical terms, these sacrifices, Christ's included, are not a matter of *propitiation* but of *expiation*. *Propitiation* carries with it the idea of appeasement, the turning away of wrath with an offering. While *propitiation* has to do with a change in the god one is appeasing, *expiation* implies the removal of an obstacle so that one can be cleansed of sin. The emphasis is on reconciliation between estranged partners. The Greek word for expiation—*hilasterion*—can also mean the "place" where atonement takes place, the mercy seat, the cover of the Ark of the Covenant in the temple where sins are wiped out. So Romans 3:25 (above) can be translated [Christ Jesus] "whom God put forward as the *mercy seat* [place] of atonement by his blood."[58]

Fourth, it does not seem that in any aspect of Jewish atonement rituals one life is substituted for another, as the penal substitutionary view of Christ's death maintains. Even rituals that dealt with sins did not involve sins deserving of death.[59] Nor was there any sense of a magical transfer or mechanistic cleansing from sin, since none of the sacrifices were effective unless the person was genuinely repentant.

Anthony Tambasco sums up the issues as follows:

> On the Day of Atonement in the Old Testament the priest sprinkled the blood of sacrifice on the mercy seat as a symbol of God's mercy, God's graciousness in forgiving their sin, and the consequent reconsecration of

---

56 Just what this laying on of hands meant in these rituals is debated by scholars.

57 See Tambasco, *Theology of Atonement,* 69–71.

58 See Joseph A. Fitzmyer, *Romans: A New Translation and Commentary*, The Anchor Bible, vol. 33 (New York: Doubleday, 1993), 350, and Christopher Bryan, *A Preface to Romans* (New York: Oxford University Press, 2000), 104, 112.

59 See Sloyan, *Crucifixion of Jesus,* 61–62.

the people to God's service. There was no sense of God being angry or having to be appeased but rather a sense of positive divine concern and action toward Israel to help right what was wrong. In the same way, when Paul describes Christ in sacrificial terms, he envisions not a penal substitute but God's gift, who, in the name of all of us, lives a life of perfect unity with God and thereby reunites us all with God.[60]

## Transformed Lives: A Journey of Participation in the Risen Life of Christ

In his letter to the Philippians, Paul includes a poetic description of Christ's willingness to be humbled, and exhorts his followers to imitate him in this. [Christ] "emptied himself, taking the form of a slave, being born in human likeness. And being found in human form he humbled himself and became obedient to the point of death—even death on a cross" (Phil. 2:7–8). This indicates that it is the whole of Christ's life and not just the cross that is the "sacrifice" that Christ made. His willing obedience contrasts with the disobedience of the first person—Adam—who brought sin into the world through disobedience (see Rom. 5:12–21). Paul continues, "Therefore God also highly exalted him and gave him the name that is above every name, so that at the name of Jesus . . . every tongue should confess that Jesus Christ is Lord, to the glory of the Father" (Phil. 2:9–11). Christ's whole way of life ended in his willingness to abide in God's will, such that he ended up on a Roman cross. But this is not the end of the story since God exalted him and raised him up to be "Lord." It is thus Christ's *whole* journey that is the means of atonement—his humble, obedient life, his death, and his exaltation.

Furthermore, the key to Paul's entire gospel is that *we participate* in this journey.[61] The problem of sin is much greater than mere transgression of a code of purity or conduct (and therefore much more profound than anything the temple sacrifices could eradicate). Rather, sin is

---

60 Tambasco, *Theology of Atonement*, 70–71.

61 See Baker and Green, *Recovering the Scandal*, 88–89, Tambasco, *Theology of Atonement*, 72–75, and Sanders, *Very Short Introduction*, 92–94.

*Sin has permeated so badly that atonement isn't just Christ's death, it's living like Him to break those sin bonds*

a *power* that enslaves us and from which we must be freed.[62] Thus, the key to our salvation lies in our own death and resurrection in Christ, signified in baptism.

> Do you not know that all of us who have been baptized into Christ Jesus were baptized into his death? Therefore we have been buried with him by baptism into death, so that, just as Christ was raised from the dead by the glory of the Father, so we too might walk in newness of life. For if we have been united with him in a death like his, we will certainly be united with him in a resurrection like his. We know that our old self was crucified with him so that the body of sin might be destroyed, and we might no longer be enslaved to sin. (Rom. 6:3–6)

This participation results in a transformation of life that is counter-cultural yet ever new. In Galatians Paul was able to say, "I have been crucified with Christ; and it is no longer I who live, but it is Christ who lives in me. And the life I now live in the flesh I live by faith in the Son of God, who loved me and gave himself up for me" (Gal. 2:19b–20). In his second letter to the Corinthians, Paul insists that, unlike Moses who had to see God with a veil over his face, for believers this veil is removed. Further, it is the Spirit who is transforming us "from one degree of glory to another" (2 Cor. 3:18). This creates a discontinuity between the "outer nature" that is wasting away and the "inner nature" that is being "renewed day by day" (2 Cor. 4:16–17). This renewal means that "from now on . . . we regard no one from a human point of view" since "if anyone is in Christ, there is a new creation; everything old has passed away; see, everything has become new" (2 Cor. 5:16–17).

This new creation exists now and yet clearly for Paul has a future consummation. His earliest letter, to the Thessalonians, is full of exhortations and promises about the return of the Lord. But there he gives few details except to say that both those who have fallen asleep and those who are still alive will be "caught up in the clouds" to "meet the Lord in the air" and "be with the Lord forever" (1 Thess. 4:17). At the end of his first letter to the Corinthians, Paul gives a more extended picture of the

---

62 See Sanders, *Very Short Introduction*, 93.

connection between this life and the next.[63] But our future transformation is entirely tied to the same transformation that took place in Christ's resurrection. Christ as risen from the dead is the "first fruits," the last Adam who, in contrast to the first Adam, is a life-giving spirit (1 Cor. 15:20–22, 45–49). We, too, will follow this trajectory: "As was the man of dust [Adam], so are those who are of the dust; and as is the man of heaven [Christ], so are those who are of heaven. Just as we have borne the image of the man of dust, we will also bear the image of the man of heaven" (1 Cor. 15:48–49). Just as Christ's resurrection was much more than resuscitation, so our resurrection will transform us from perishable flesh and blood to an imperishable body.[64]

Exactly what this will "look like" Paul could not say—he refers to it as a mystery. Nevertheless he waxes eloquent in a now famous passage about death and transformation:

> Listen, I will tell you a mystery! We will not all die, but we will all be changed, in a moment, in the twinkling of an eye, at the last trumpet. For the trumpet will sound, and the dead will be raised imperishable, and we will be changed. For this perishable body must put on imperishability, and this mortal body must put on immortality . . . then the saying that is written will be fulfilled: "Death has been swallowed up in victory. Where, O death, is your victory? Where, O death, is your sting?" The sting of death is sin, and the power of sin is the law. But thanks be to God, who gives us the victory through our Lord Jesus Christ. (1 Cor. 15:51–57)

In conclusion, according to Paul, not only is the means of atonement with God much more than a narrow substitution of one life (Christ's) for another (ours), it involves the whole of Christ's pattern of life in God. Most important, atonement is not merely an objective "status" that Christ

---

63 For more on resurrection in 1 Corinthians 15, see Tambasco, *Theology of Atonement*, 81–85. For the role of the Holy Spirit, see ibid., 85–90.

64 Note that Paul insists on some kind of new *body*. The gospel witness is that Jesus had a new body and was not a ghost. Likewise, whatever comes after death, it is not about immortality of the *soul* but about a new existence that involves *bodies*. See Bryan, *The Resurrection of the Messiah*, chaps. 1 and 2. For an argument that this is a properly Jewish idea and not new with Christians, see Jon D. Levensen, *Resurrection and the Restoration of Israel: The Ultimate Victory of the God of Life* (New Haven, CT: Yale University Press, 2006).

has somehow won for us through his death. Rather, it is *our entire life* as participating in Christ's death and resurrection, symbolized in baptism. It is not that Christ reconciled us to God (way back when) and we now enjoy benefits. Rather Christ himself was transformed to a new humanity in his resurrection and we are transformed likewise into a new way of being ourselves. This new way of being will have a future of further transformation. But so far from being a ticket out of hell, this further transformation will only draw us deeper into the life of God, a life we already share.

## Conclusion

We have delved deeply into recent and reputable New Testament scholarship in order to grasp what it means to say that Jesus died for our sins. We can safely affirm that the New Testament witnesses—those recording Jesus's embodied, spoken, and symbolic meanings, along with Paul in his letters—consistently assert that Jesus's life, death, and resurrection was "for us." Furthermore, they insist that this "for us" involves our ultimate destiny with God and our ongoing participation in God's revolutionary work in the world. Just how Jesus's being for us functions is never pinned down systematically. Rather, a host of metaphors and allusions—from ransom to justification to redemption to mercy seat or Day of Atonement—are elicited. No one metaphor takes pride of place or is privileged over another. Likewise the "us" for whom Jesus has won salvation is sometimes the people of God, sometimes the entire human race, and at other times the entire cosmos or whole created order. While there is certainly the idea that Jesus stood as a representative of humankind in suffering the judgment of God as a catalyst for an entirely new order, the idea that God punished Jesus in our place in order to realign some universal scheme of justice whereby sin required a violent response is not supported.

*Again, I don't believe these are mutually exclusive ideas*

*You didn't disprove a violent response, you just gave an alternative*

# 3

# From Metaphor to Theory

## Further Attempts to Make Sense of What God Has Done in Christ

In the last chapter we stressed that the earliest Christians, in their preaching and writing, relied on images and metaphors to convey the sense they had that God had done something dramatically new in Christ. Furthermore, these metaphorical references were multiple and varied. *Justification*—being made righteous before God—implied a court of law. *Redemption* had economical overtones. *Sacrifice* came from the world of worship. *Reconciliation* had to do with personal relations. *Triumph over evil* brought to mind the battlefield and *adoption* had to do with family structures.[1] In simplest form the point is that none of

---

1 See Mark D. Baker and Joel B. Green, *Recovering the Scandal of the Cross: Atonement in New Testament and Contemporary Contexts*, 2nd ed. (Downers Grove, IL: InterVarsity Press, 2011), 123–34, and Stephen Finlan, *Options on Atonement in Christian Thought* (Collegeville, MN: Liturgical Press, 2007), 1.

these constitute attempts to give a systematic account of how the Christ event changed the human-divine relationship. While systematic theologies eventually emerged, a wide variety of approaches is apparent not only in the New Testament but also in the centuries that followed.

It is impossible here to provide a complete history of interpretations of salvation or the cross in Christian history. Even a cursory review would not do justice to the wide variety of traditions that have developed around Christian convictions that God in Christ was saving the world from sin and its consequences.[2] The focus of this chapter will be the work of Anselm, archbishop of Canterbury, considered the first to shift his approach away from metaphor to a more systematic account of salvation. However, we will first indicate a few of the proposals that preceded him. We will also say something about popular piety up to and through the Middle Ages, in which the cross of Christ and his suffering became prominent.

# A Patristic Sampling

For the most part the variety and metaphorical approach of the first century CE continued in the centuries after the New Testament writings were complete. Just as the New Testament writers were all responding to concrete circumstances that demanded pastoral attention, so the *patristic* writers—the "fathers" of the church—wrote letters and treatises in response to their circumstances. Sometimes these writers addressed non-believers but most often, as was the case for Paul, they were concerned with other Christians who were misinterpreting the meaning of Christ's entrance into the world. A review of Christianity in the early centuries reveals a plethora of Christiani*ties*. It was this diversity that instigated debates among bishops and theologians over who, exactly, Christ was, particularly with regard to his humanity and divinity. While the nature and means of salvation were not theologically front and center in these debates, it was clear to all of those involved that nothing less than

---

2 With regard to the cross and how it has been viewed through early Christian history, see Elizabeth Dreyer, ed., *The Cross in Christian Tradition: From Paul to Bonaventure* (New York: Paulist Press, 2000). See also Gerard S. Sloyan, *The Crucifixion of Jesus: History, Myth, Faith* (Minneapolis: Fortress Press, 1995). This chapter will rely on this latter book, especially chapters 4, 5, and 7.

redemption itself was at stake. Who Jesus was and what he accomplished for us are irretrievably interwoven.

Given this diversity we can nevertheless make a few general statements about salvation as viewed by believers in the century after the New Testament writings were completed. On the one hand, it is notable that the graphic details of Jesus's death on a Roman cross went unmentioned and were left obscure, as was, for the most part, true in the New Testament accounts of his death. On the other hand, it is clear that the notion that "Jesus died for our sins" continued to play a central role, and that this dying for our sins was taken to refer to a cultic event. There were the Jewish precedents in the temple sacrifices and the Day of Atonement ritual of Leviticus 16. In addition, the cultural world of the Mediterranean basin was saturated with cults that engaged in ritual sacrifices. Thus, though crucifixion is not a notably bloody form of execution, references to blood came to be used as a substitute for cross early on, indicating the ritual significance of Jesus's death.

That believers gathered regularly, in a variety of venues and under a wide spectrum of circumstances, is well documented. It is likewise clear that when they gathered they invariably celebrated the rituals that Jesus had left for them: baptizing new believers and sharing bread and wine as symbols of his body and blood which was shed for them. The cross event thus was transposed to *cultus*—a set of actions with accompanying meanings that left historical detail and description to the side. With the destruction of the temple in Jerusalem by the Romans in 70 CE even Jewish worship had shifted to a spirituality of sacrifice in a nonliteralist mode. Repeated sacrifices such as those employed in pagan cults were clearly off-limits for Christians since they embodied an idolatry that could not be tolerated.[3] For Christians, ritual sacrifice in its literal mode had occurred once and for all in the events of Calvary. They celebrated the fruits of this sacrifice on a regular basis by partaking of the body and blood of the Lord in the eucharistic meal.

Gerard Sloyan draws this conclusion:

> From the New Testament times to the third quarter of the second century the prevailing Christian conviction was that humanity was bought back or ransomed from the

---

3 That the question arose is evidenced by Paul's need to address it in 1 Corinthians 6–8.

guilt of sin by Jesus' sacrifice (his "blood"), much as
God accepted the blood of beasts and birds as vicarious
of human life. There was no theorizing on whether
Christ's blood was an actual purchase price and, if
so, paid to whom. Faith in the offering of his life was
sufficient to bring total release from sin on the last day,
but an upright life was the condition of this faith. . . .
His death had acquired the status of a rite, universal and
cosmic in its effects.[4]

Irenaeus (125–200) was bishop of Lyons in current-day France. Born
in Asia Minor he had studied under Polycarp, who, tradition has it, had
himself been a disciple of John the Evangelist. Irenaeus faced serious
pastoral problems when, after a set of particularly bloody persecutions
in Lyons, he was made bishop and had to deal with a church in dis-
array. This chaos was not helped by the Gnostic Christians who were
vying for the loyalty of the Christian minority in the district. Gnosticism
was a philosophy/religion that embraced the Greek notion of a dualism
between matter and spirit, mind and body. This view asserted that the
problem of human existence, the source of evil in the world, had to do
with embodied existence. The human spirit needed to be released from
its captivity in material bodies. This came through enlightenment—special knowledge (*gnosis*) from the gods. The Christian version of this saw
the Christ—the Word of God—as an emissary of light, bringing new
knowledge to those in bondage to physical, corruptible existence. But
these Christians had little interest in the historical Jesus and, furthermore, discounted the humanity of Christ altogether.

Iraneaus had little patience for this group. In 180 he wrote *Adversus
Haereses* (Against Heresies) to confront such wrong-headed ideas. He
wanted to counteract the Gnostic denial of the Incarnation. For him, it
was essential to believe that Christ was *both* human and divine. When
it came to salvation, the issue was not one of "getting out of" human
embodiment. The problem of evil lay not in matter itself, but in Adam's
willing disobedience of God in the garden of Eden (Gen. 3). This disobedience left the human race devoid of the image of God that had been its
original identity. In the Incarnation Christ *recapitulated* the creation of
the human race, so that our God-likeness might be restored.

---

4 Sloyan, *Crucifixion of Jesus,* 104.

*Jesus' birth atonement*

> When [the son of God] became incarnate, and was made
> man, he recapitulated in himself the long line of human
> beings. He obtained salvation for us in miniature so that
> what we lost in Adam, namely our being in the image
> and likeness of God, might be recovered in Jesus Christ.[5]

Thus, for Irenaeus, redemption occurred as a result of the Incarnation. In a world of Platonic thought, the notion of humankind as a universal reality would have been common. That Adam represented this universal, taking the whole of humankind into corruptibility, would have made sense. Likewise, the idea of Christ suffusing all of humanity with immortality and thus redeeming the entire race, would not have seemed odd.

Still, for Irenaeus it was not just the Incarnation that saved us; the whole of Christ's life, death, and resurrection is involved:

> So, if He was not born, neither did He die; and if He did
> not die, neither was He raised from the dead; and if He
> was not raised from the dead, He has not conquered death,
> nor is its reign abolished; and if death is not conquered,
> how are we to mount on high into life, being subject from
> the beginning to death?[6]

WHAT?

Irenaeus also incorporates a motif he inherited from Scripture and that will carry great weight in the patristic period: that of a struggle with the devil, leading to the ultimate victory of Christ. Jesus had a lifelong struggle with the devil, beginning in the desert and ending with the passion, which was contrived by the devil himself. Christ's blood ransoms humankind from the power of the devil; Christ seems to be defeated on the cross but, by handing himself over willingly, in the end he becomes the victor.

The notions of ransom and release would have been powerful images in the early centuries of Christianity. Marauding gangs roamed the countryside, pillaging property and kidnapping travelers. Conquering powers

---

5 *Adversus Haereses* 3.18.1, as quoted in Sloyan, *Crucifixion of Jesus,* 105. For another translation, see http://www.newadvent.org/fathers/0103318.htm. Accessed June 1, 2015.

6 Irenaeus, *Proof of the Apostolic Preaching,* 39, as quoted in Baker and Green, *Recovering the Scnadal,* 146. See alternative translation at http://www.tertullian.org/fathers/irenaeus_02_proof.htm. Accessed June 1, 2015.

in political struggles would take slaves as the spoils of war. Paul had talked of being enslaved to sin in his letters, and the idea that Adam's sin had left humankind in slavery to the devil—the tempter and accuser—captured believers' imaginations. The nature of this enslavement to the devil, and just what transpired when the ransom was paid, eventually became the subject of much debate.

Origen of Alexandria (ca. 185–254) was the first to develop this motif at length. In answer to the question, "To whom was the ransom paid?" he answered that it could not be to God, so it must have been to "the evil one." "For he had power over us until the ransom given to him on our behalf, namely the life of Jesus; and he was deceived thinking that he could keep his soul in power."[7] Gregory of Nyssa (330–ca. 395) is most famous for the image of the devil being "baited" by the "hook" of Christ's humanity: "God therefore hid himself under the veil of our nature so that the devil, throwing himself like a ravenous fish on the bait of mankind, might be caught on the hook of Deity."[8] Since, in fact, Christ was divine, the devil could not in the end hold him. The devil was thus tricked by God while God won out in the end. The Incarnation remains central here, since it was Christ's divinity that exposed the devil's cunning and that freed humankind from its bondage to sin and the evil one.[9]

The imagery of deceiving the devil and the motif of *Christus Victor* carried psychic power even though they raised difficulties theologically.[10] The most basic difficulty was the idea that God and the devil were somehow equal partners in an exchange, that God in some way "owed" something to the devil. Augustine of Hippo (354–430) modified the motif in a number of ways. He did this by acknowledging that the

---

7 Origen is commenting on Matthew 20:28—" a ransom for many." *In Matthaeum* 16.8 (translation from Henry Bettenson, ed., *The Early Christian Fathers* [Oxford: Oxford University Press, 1956], 224), as quoted in Baker and Green, *Recovering the Scandal*, 147.

8 Gregory of Nyssa, *Great Catechism* 24, as quoted in Sloyan, *Crucifixion of Jesus*, 109. See, alternatively, http://www.ccel.org/ccel/schaff/npnf205.xi.ii.xxvi.html. Accessed June 1, 2015.

9 See Sloyan, *Crucifixion of Jesus*, 108–10.

10 The classic book that brought this motif to light in recent scholarship is Gustaf Aulen, *Christus Victor: An Historical Study of the Three Main Types of the Idea of Atonement*, trans. A. G. Hebert (New York: MacMillan, 1969). Even more recently this model of atonement has been rehabilitated by books such as Darby Kathleen Ray, *Deceiving the Devil: Atonement, Abuse, and Ransom* (Cleveland: Pilgrim Press, 1998), and J. Denny Weaver, *The Nonviolent Atonement*, 2nd ed. (Grand Rapids, MI: Eerdmans, 2011).

devil did indeed have a "kind of divine justice" in his power over the human race. But any power he had was not strictly just but was granted to him only by God's permission. The heart of human sin lies in the lust for power, and the devil—the deceiver—is the epitome of this power mongering. In choosing to worship power Adam had committed the human race to the dominion of the prince of deceit. God had allowed this because he gave humankind freedom of choice.[11]

The devil does, then, have a "just" claim, in that Adam (humankind) did indeed sin. But the devil overreaches his power in claiming that he has rights that need to be adjudicated. His appeal to justice—his right to a ransom—is a mere cover story for his own "power grab." Augustine is quite clear on the injustice of the deceiver's claim. God in no way is bound by it.

The key to Augustine's position is to recognize that God, in Christ, chose not to beat the devil through a power play. Instead, God restores justice and order. Justice wins the day, not power.

> But the devil would have to be overcome not by God's power but by his justice. What, after all, could be more powerful than the all-powerful, or what creature power could compare with the creator's? The essential flaw of the devil's perversion made him a lover of power and a deserter and assailant of justice, which means that men imitate him all the more thoroughly the more they neglect or even detest justice and studiously devote themselves to power. . . . So it pleased God to deliver man from the devil's authority by beating him at the justice game, not the power game, so that men too might imitate Christ by seeking to beat the devil at the justice game, not the power game.[12]

How is it that Christ accomplishes this? It was precisely through his choice to share with us in our death even though he was under no obligation to do so. Though he was the sinless one, free of anything that the

---

11 Augustine, *The Trinity*, ed. John E. Rotelle, trans. Edmund Hill. *The Works of Saint Augustine: A Translation for the 21st Century*, part I, vol. 5 (New York: New York City Press, 1991). See book 13, chaps. 19–20.

12 Ibid., 13,17; p. 356.

*I don't agree*

devil might use to manipulate or accuse him, he nevertheless surrendered to the devil's contrived execution.

> What then is the justice that overpowered the devil? The justice of Jesus Christ—what else? And how was he overpowered? He found nothing in him deserving of death and yet he killed him. It is therefore perfectly just that he should let the debtors he held go free, who believe in the one whom he killed without his [Christ] being in his [the devil's] debt.[13]

When the devil discovered that there was nothing in Jesus actually deserving of death, yet killed him anyway, the devil's cover was blown. He was not, in fact, concerned with justice, but only with his own power. The lie exposed, the devil's power to accuse is broken. There is perhaps a measure of "trickery" here, but it is all on the part of the deceiver. Concerned only with power, he cannot conceive of a human agent who is not as power hungry as he is. He is thus tricked—or at least surprised—when confronted with Christ's loving surrender.

In sum, the earliest Christians continued to hold that "Jesus died for our sins" was central to their faith. They did this by participating in Christ's death and resurrection through baptism and the recurrent ritual of the Eucharist. The ensuing centuries reveal theologians bound to the efficacy of the Incarnation—that a new Adam had "recapitulated" the old Adam who was bound to sin, death, and the evil one. Christ's death served as a sort of ransom to the devil, though it took Augustine to insist that this was not a just payment. Indeed, there was captivity and bondage. Certainly Christ's death served as a release from this enslavement. But the heart of the matter lay in Christ's sinlessness and his willingness to yield himself to the devil's power, revealing the devil's claims to justice to be fraudulent. This freed sinners from the devil's grip and offered them a model to follow.

# Anselm and Satisfaction

Anselm of Canterbury (1033–1109) is the theologian to whom many

---

13 Ibid., 13,18; p. 357.

contemporary scholars point when outlining the problems with a violent atonement theory. He is credited with codifying the theory of a transaction whereby Christ stood in for us so that we might not suffer the punishment that was our due because of sin. For this reason, Anselm deserves our special attention here. We need to clarify just what he did and did not advocate, and to discover what parts of his theory may be worth retaining today.

By the time we get to Anselm in Christian history, we are a long, long way from the cultural worlds in which Irenaeus, Gregory of Nyssa, or Augustine of Hippo lived and wrote. In the meantime, the conversion of Constantine to Christianity (312) had engendered Christendom, a world in which Christian faith became the cultural norm. In the century after Constantine, the Roman Empire gradually fell apart and Christian leaders stepped into the chaos, establishing the authority of the church for centuries to come. By the tenth century, when Anselm was born, the church was central to any and all social order, and the Christian faith was presumed to be the norm of civilization. Monastic life was well established and a mainstay of literate and cultural life.

Anselm was born in 1033 in the town of Aosta in northern Italy.[14] From an early age he was attracted to monastic life, but postponed his search for a monastic home until after his mother's death in 1056. At this point Anselm left Italy and wandered north, looking for a place to study. The great universities of Europe would not be fully established until the next century, so a quest for learning led Anselm to the monastery of Bec in Normandy. He was drawn there in hopes of studying with the renowned scholar Lanfranc. He embraced the full monastic life in 1060, three years later replacing Lanfranc as prior, and then fifteen years later becoming abbot. In 1093 Anselm was called to be archbishop of Canterbury, a post he held until he died, and a post fraught with difficulty due to tensions with the British monarchs under which he served.

Throughout his years of ecclesiastical duties, Anselm continued to write and he has left a legacy of scholarship. His conflicts with King William Rufus led him into and out of exile from England over a number of years. It was one such exile in Padua, Italy, in the summer of 1098 that

---

14 This section relies in part on William P. Loewe, *Lex Crucis: Soteriology and the Stages of Meaning* (Minneapolis: Fortress Press, 2016), chap. 2.

brought Anselm welcome relief from ecclesiastical turmoil. It was here that he was able to turn his attention to his treatise *Cur Deus Homo?*

*Cur Deus Homo?* means "Why Did God Become Human?" In chapter 1 of book I of this treatise, Anselm expands on the question: "By what logic or necessity did God become man, and by his death, as we believe and profess, restore life to the world, when he could have done this through the agency of some other person, angelic or human, or simply by willing it?"[15] His reference here to "logic or necessity" is important because Anselm marks a departure from the methods by which salvation had been appropriated up to that point. Whereas previous authors had left a rich legacy of images and themes, Anselm wants to develop arguments that could appeal to nonbelievers, based on reason more than narratives or metaphors.

In I,3 Anselm rehearses some typologies that his predecessors had used. Just as sin came through a human, so also salvation came from a human. This is the recapitulation notion from St. Paul and Irenaeus. Further, in each case a woman was involved; Eve as temptress to Adam and Mary as the "originator of our justification." Finally, just as the first sinner was tempted by fruit on a tree, so salvation was won through Christ hanging on a tree. While Anselm acknowledges a certain beauty in these corresponding typologies, he thinks they need a more solid ground on which to stand. Anselm wants more than *convenientiae,* appropriate images. He appeals instead to *ratio et necessitas* (reason and necessity): "What has to be demonstrated, therefore, is the logical soundness of the truth, that is: cogent reason which proves that God ought to have, or could have, humbled himself for the purposes which we proclaim."[16]

The format by which Anselm undertakes this task is a dialogue. He creates an interlocutor in the person of Boso, a younger monk who presses Anselm to provide precisely the reasoning that Anselm has advocated. Furthermore, in the quest for a reasoned position, Anselm explains to Boso at the outset that he wants to argue in a way that an unbeliever would understand. In other words, book 1 is undertaken to argue *as if* one did not know Christ and the salvation he has wrought. Once Anselm has

15 Anselm of Canterbury, *Anselm of Canterbury: The Major Works,* Oxford World Classics (Oxford: Oxford University Press, 1998), 265. References in text will refer to either book 1 or 2, with chapter numbers following. Footnotes will refer to book, chapter, and then pages in this edition.

16 Ibid., I,4, p. 269.

presented the problem—of the human race under the reign of sin—and outlined what its logical solution must be—an offering of someone both human and divine—then he can, in book II, show that this solution finds its reality in Christ incarnate.

So what is Anselm's line of reasoning? He takes for granted that his readers understand that there *is* a problem, which is sin and the alienation that it has wrought between God and humankind. Anselm refines this by discussing God's honor as being violated by human failure to give God what God is owed, namely worship and thanksgiving. This violation needs to be redressed. God's honor can be restored through the punishment of death, which is merited by human sin. The only other way to restore God's honor would be through some act of recompense, or *satisfaction,* whereby a deed above and beyond what is already owed to God could be given to God.

The logical problem is that this offering must be on the part of a human agent, since it is humans who have sinned, while at the same time the offering must *go beyond* what humans have to offer, since the offense is of such great proportion. Humankind has nothing to offer God that they have not already received from God. There is nothing "more" they can give in order to repair the breach. Christ's giving of his life is exactly this something "more." Christ was human so he acts as a human agent in seeking reconciliation with God. Yet Christ as God was under no obligation to give his life. Since he was sinless, death would not have come to him. That he willingly gave his life as an act of obedient love is what constitutes satisfaction and wins us reconciliation with the one we have offended. The punishment of death is remitted without injustice.

So the short answer to "Why did God become man?" is that only a God-man could offer a complete recompense for sin. The logic of the problem in book I comes to the conclusion that the way out of the sin dilemma is either the punishment of death or some offering beyond what humans already owe to God. Since humankind is incapable of the latter, the logic leads one to despair: it seems that there is no way out except punishment and death. The incarnation of the God-man Christ resolves this, not in the incarnation alone but in the willingness of the God-man to suffer what he in no way deserved. This, then, becomes the "over and above" gift—what is *supererogatory*—by which God offers back to humankind the merit of salvation.

There are several key points in this argument that must be drawn
out carefully if we are to understand exactly what Anselm was up to,
and to grasp that he was not about some kind of substitutionary punishment. First, we need to grasp the notion of God's *honor*. Scholars
point out that Anselm is working in a world of feudal aristocracy, one
in which each person has his or her role to play within a carefully designated hierarchy. In this world, to step outside one's place would indeed
be a matter of terrible indiscretion.

However, the important point is not so much that those in the
upper echelons of this hierarchy—the lords—will "take offense" in the
modern sense of "be offended." Rather, the issue is the disruption of
an entire system of governance and meaning. God's honor is not some
upper-class snobbery that needs placating. In the way Anselm means it,
it is the entire system of "right order" which human sin disrupts. The
modern analogy would *not* be that of the teacher or parent or coach who
takes offense when a teenager spouts off vulgarities in challenging his
or her authority. While this action might indeed require just redress, the
better image would be that of recent events in Syria, or the Ukraine, or
even the genocide in Rwanda. These are situations of complete disorder
when sin leads to disruption of the social milieu. Chaos, confusion, the
inability to get back to basic mistakes that need repair; all of this is what
sin produces. *This* is the magnitude of what goes wrong when "God's
honor"—God's ordering and mankind's grateful and humble response—
gets "broken."[17]

Second, the key to understanding Anselm's soteriology is the dis-
junction—*aut poena, aut satisfactio. Either* punishment *or* satisfaction.[18] Anselm says:

> For—setting aside the fact that God does many good things,
> in all manner of ways, for the benefit of wrong-doers—
> the alternatives, voluntary recompense [*satisfactio*] for
> wrongdoing, or the exaction of punishment [*poena*] from

---

17 Note that Anselm recognizes the limits of his analogy in that while the feudal system might
break down if honor is breached, Anselm insists that God's honor stands independent of
the vagaries of human response. In the bigger picture, while sin and disorder may reign
supreme in temporal existence, God's order can never be fully abrogated by human action.
See I,14–15, pp. 287–89.

18 For more on this point, see Charles Hefling, "A Perhaps Permanently Valid Achievement:
Lonergan and Christ's Satisfaction," *Method: Journal of Lonergan Studies* 10 (1992), 51–76.

someone who does not give recompense, retain their own proper place in this same universal order and their own regulatory beauty.[19]

The point is that satisfaction is not punishment. Christ did offer satisfaction—recompense—as a compensation for loss suffered. And he did this on our behalf, indeed as a substitute for us since we were incapable of such a compensation. But he did it *as an alternative to* punishment. Because of this offering, humankind is not punished. But it is not the case, according to Anselm, that we are *not* punished because Christ *was* punished.

Anselm is indeed concerned that God's justice must be upheld. And in keeping with much of New Testament teaching he believes that God's justice is *retributive*; God demands recourse for human sin. It is also the case, though Anselm is careful to nuance what this means, that God intended Christ to die. So Charles Hefling comes to the basic dilemma and Anselm's careful answer:

> If God is just, if there is a divine justice that is retributive, and if God willed the suffering and death of Christ, then was the cross an act of divine retribution?
>
> That it was is exactly the conclusion which Anselm's theory of satisfaction manages to avoid. With Anselm the justice that has to be satisfied is God's justice to himself. It would be unjust to allow divine honor to remain violated. Punishing the violator, the human race, would restore it; so would an unowed gift. But it has to be one or the other. The two possibilities are strictly alternative. That is one way in which the key to *Cur Deus Homo* lies in the disjunction *aut satisfactio aut poena*, either satisfaction or else punishment, since it allows Anselm to hold that in no sense was Christ punished by God. On the contrary, the satisfaction he made consisted wholly in performing a deed which was above and beyond human obligation towards God, and which honored God precisely because God did not require him to perform it.[20]

---

19 Anselm, I,15, p. 289.
20 Hefling, "Perhaps Permanently Valid Achievement," 60.

In other words, quite contrary to the view with which Anselm is often credited, his theory of satisfaction is not about substitutionary punishment.

A third important aspect of Anselm's position is the free offering that Christ made in living his life to such fullness that it resulted in his death. Anselm is at pains to insist that although Christ's gift is one of obedience, it is not something that is forced upon him by God. This is tied to the fact that Christ was without sin and therefore was not subject to death. Anselm puts it thus:

> God, therefore did not force Christ to die, there being no sin in him. Rather he underwent death of his own accord, not out of an obedience consisting in the abandonment of his life, but out of an obedience consisting in his upholding of righteousness so bravely and pertinaciously that as a result he incurred death.[21]

Several points merge here. Christ did not deserve death since he did not sin. Christ nevertheless freely chose to die, though in "choosing death" he was in fact choosing to live a life that would result in death. This willingly offered death constitutes an offering to God that is *supererogatory,* that is, over and above what humankind already owed to God as creatures. The Father in receiving this gift allows the reward he then owes to the Son to be bestowed instead on humankind in the remission of punishment for sin.[22]

The significance of this willing death of Christ cannot be overstated. It is important because it means that the essence of salvation—what in philosophical terms we would call its *formal cause*—lies not in the death itself but in Christ's loving willingness to die. Salvation for Anselm is not a matter of *death* but of loving obedience.[23] Once again, death as a violent act, though surely an element in Christ's work of salvation, is not its heart.

---

21 Anselm, I,9, p. 277.

22 See Anselm, II,18–19, pp. 348–54.

23 Thomas Aquinas, in the next century, will take up Anselm's notion of satisfaction and integrate it into his wider systematic theology in the *Summa Theologiae.* In this case Aquinas makes Christ's love—*caritas*—the whole, not a part, of his work of salvation. Giles Mongeau makes this point in his unpublished paper, "Aquinas' Theology of the Cross." On charity in general in Aquinas, see the *Summa Theologiae*, the second part of the second part (IIaIIae), articles 23–33. On the passion and what it accomplished, see ibid., the third part (IIIa), questions 46–49.

In sum, read carefully, Anselm's theory of satisfaction is not the culprit when it comes to atonement understood as a violent act perpetrated on one person of the Trinity by another. Anselm does place a great deal of importance on the justice of God, which is not justice in the narrow sense of court proceedings but in the broad sense of the order of creation whereby God providently governs. Anselm's term for this providential divine ordering is God's "honor." Anselm likewise takes sin extremely seriously and insists that it cannot go unremitted; this would violate God's very nature. But Anselm's explanation of the divine solution to the human problem lies directly contrary to the idea that God sent his Son to die in our stead. The incarnation of the Son, and the full humanity of Christ, is essential to his position. But the heart of what Christ offered to God for our sins lies in his loving obedience, his life freely lived in spite of its trajectory toward death, a death in no way deserved. It is by this unowed gift of loving obedience, not his death per se, that Christ wins salvation for humankind.

# Popular Piety and the Sufferings of Christ

Anselm's shift to arguments by "reason and necessity" mark a shift in soteriology to *theory*—an attempt to explain God's work of salvation independent of our experience of it. This mode of discourse will continue in the centuries to come. However, we need to acknowledge that the use of metaphors and symbolic meaning with regard to Christ's death—*cultus* in the broadest sense—continues apace. While reasoned argument seeks explanations that put logic into the relations between the human and the divine, and within and among the persons of the Trinity, reasoned arguments can fail to capture the hearts and minds of believers. Thus it is worth our while to trace very briefly some ways in which the cross became central in Christian devotion, particularly in the Middle Ages.

There are artifacts showing that the image of a cross was used in the early church, either empty or with a figure of some kind on it.[24] Both Tertullian (160–225) in Latin and Origen (ca. 185–264) in Greek mention

---

24 For concrete examples, see Sloyan, *Crucifixion of Jesus,* 124–27.

that Christians would trace a "T" on their foreheads before beginning prayer or work. Constantine evidently introduced the practice of tracing a cross on shields before battle. In addition, Eusebius, his biographer, recounts how the emperor erected a sign of the Lord's passion "decorated with gold and precious stones" in a prominent place in his palace.[25]

Prior to Constantine there had been multiple, if sporadic, persecutions, so that martyrdom was hailed as an ideal for the life of faith. These martyrs saw themselves as following in Jesus's footsteps. The desert hermits also envisioned themselves as taking on a life of hardship in imitation of Jesus. Gerard Sloyan draws the conclusion:

> The preaching and teaching of the patristic period . . . was marked by two features in particular: an invitation to emulate his innocent suffering by accepting the trials of life as a witness to him and an emphasis on the fact that the divine Man who was the framer of the universe had freely subjected himself to the indignities of his human tormentors. There was stress neither on the physical pain he endured nor on seeking out suffering quite like his as reparatory.[26]

Moving on to the early medieval period, Nathan D. Mitchell analyzes the centrality of the cross in worship in the tenth century, illustrated by the Good Friday liturgy of the *Regularis Concordia*. This was a code drawn up to regularize monastic life in "the English nation" in the late 900s, part of what is often called "the English monastic revival of the tenth century."[27] The Good Friday liturgy consisted of three parts: (1) the Liturgy of the Word, culminating in a solemn reading of the passion from John's Gospel, (2) veneration of the cross, and (3) a celebration of the Eucharist. What is notable, according to Mitchell, is the way in which the liturgy had become a *drama* in its own right. During the reading of the Gospel, two deacons are instructed to act "like thieves" and strip the altar of the cloth that lies under the Gospel, just as the story tells of the Roman guards dividing Jesus's garments among them.

---

25 Eusebius, *Life of Constantine* 3.49, as quoted in Sloyan, *Crucifixion of Jesus,* 126. See also http://www.newadvent.org/fathers/25023.htm. Accessed June 1, 2015.

26 Sloyan, *Crucifixion of Jesus* 129.

27 Nathan D. Mitchell, "The Cross That Spoke," in Dreyer, *Cross,* 72–92, esp. 73.

After the Gospel reading and the prayers, the veneration of the cross begins when the veil that has covered it is taken off and the cross is laid on a cushion before the altar. The instructions continue:

> As soon as it has been unveiled the abbot shall come before the holy Cross and shall prostrate himself thrice with all the brethren of the right hand side of the choir, that is, seniors and juniors; and with deep and heartfelt sighs shall say the seven penitential psalms and the prayers in honor of the holy Cross.[28]

This Good Friday liturgy illustrates how liturgy had shifted from being a priestly ritual to "a kind of dramatic tableau in which past historical events are reenacted."[29] For New Testament authors and patristic theologians, the cross was an event with cosmic significance, with the focus being on the outcome, namely salvation for sinners. By the early Middle Ages, the cross had become an object of worship in its own right:

In sum, the cross, as understood by Paul or John or the author of Hebrews

> is the symbolic nexus of a whole set of relationships that define and connect Christ and the Christian, Jew and Greek, past and present, source and sacrament, cult and culture. In the *Regularis Concordia,* however, a rather different ideology seems to be at work. For by the tenth century (and indeed much before), the cross had become a cult object in its own right, worthy of acclamation, address and adoration—worthy, in short, of *liturgy.* The cross is no longer just a soteriological event, a theological outcome or even a prop in a monastic drama. Rather, it has become a central *character* with a speaking role of its own. It can be hailed, held, clothed and greeted like any other character.[30]

---

28 *Regularis Concordia: The Monastic Agreement of the Monks and Nuns in the English Nation*, ed. Thomas Symons (New York: Thomas Nelson and Sons, 1953), 43, as quoted in Mitchell, "Cross," in Dreyer, *Cross*, 75.

29 Mitchell, "Cross," in Dreyer, *Cross*, 74.

30 Ibid., 76.

Furthermore, by the early Middle Ages, the method of *lectio divina*—the slow reading and meditating on the Bible in private—led to the monastic practice of identifying with Jesus and a desire to emulate him in his sufferings. Even Anselm, in spite of his detached reasoning in *Cur Deus Homo?,* summoned the Crucified in his imagination and addressed his prayers to him:

> Kindlest, gentlest most serene Lord,
> will you not make it up to me for not seeing
> the blessed incorruption of your flesh,
> for not having kissed the place of the wounds
>     where the nails pierced,
> for not having sprinkled with tears of joy
> the scars that prove the truth of your body?[31]

This devotion to the crucified Jesus had been common among groups of nuns and devout women called canonesses for several centuries. The practices of these women indicate an early medieval devotion to Christ's wounds, his holy face, and the spear that pierced his side.[32]

Bernard of Clairvaux (1090–1153) is seen as solidifying this devotion to Christ's humanity in Western Christian practice in the high Middle Ages. He wrote extensively in a good Latin style and incorporated into his writings a disclosure of sentiments. An expression of affectivity was just beginning to be accepted without embarrassment at this time. He thus encouraged loving compassion in the consideration of the sufferings of the Lord along with imitation of Christ in practices of "mortification" in one's daily duties. In a sermon he writes, "What can be so effective a cure for the wound of conscience and so purifying to keenness of mind as steady meditation on the wounds of Christ?"[33]

This tradition of meditating on the suffering of Christ reached another level in the following century with the meandering preachers

---

31 Anselm, "Prayer to Christ," as quoted in Sloyan, *Crucifixion of Jesus,* 132. For other examples of his prayers, see http://aclerkofoxford.blogspot.ca/2012/06/anselms-prayer-to-st-paul-our-greatest.html. Accessed June 1, 2015.

32 Sloyan, *Crucifixion of Jesus,* 134.

33 "Sermon 62," Bernard of Clairvaux, *Bernard of Clairvaux: Selected Works,* trans., Gillian R. Evans (New York: Paulist Press, 1987), 247, as quoted in Sloyan, *Crucifixion of Jesus,* 135. For more on Bernard, see http://en.wikipedia.org/wiki/Bernard_of_Clairvaux and http://www.osb.org/cist/bern.html. Accessed June 1, 2015.

who followed in the footsteps of Francis of Assisi (1182–1226).[34] While many *Lives* of Francis were written in the generation after his death, Francis himself drew up a *Testament* just before he died, in which he recorded that on September 17, 1224, he received the wounds of Christ on his own body. Known as "stigmata," there was no precedent for a miracle of this sort. It was understood to be a sign of his complete identification with the Lord through penance, prayer, and love. The many men and women who followed in his footsteps went throughout Europe preaching the power of this kind of identification with the human Jesus. Gerard Sloyan puts it thus: "The theory of suffering as the sole way to glory may have peaked with Bernard a century before, but no one made the infant Jesus or the Jesus who healed or suffered torment more real in people's lives than the sons and daughter of the Poverello [St. Francis]."[35]

The thirteenth century is considered the height of Christian culture in medieval Europe. St. Francis and St. Dominic started new religious orders that served God through action rather than in cloistered contemplation. Universities were now well established as centers of theological systematic teaching and writing. This was the era of St. Thomas Aquinas with his twenty-nine volumes of the *Summa Theologiae*. Religious life and theological thinking were in ascendancy.

Great tragedies were, however, on the horizon, making the late Middle Ages a very different time religiously. The Hundred Years' War between England and France (1337–1453) meant political instability while the church leadership teetered on uncertainty during the Great Western Schism, when two different papacies claimed authority (1378–1429). In the middle of all this was the Black Plague (1348–1350), when a third to a half of the population of Europe was killed, leaving social turmoil.[36] All this uncertainty left the populace anxious and superstitious. It also left them clinging to any devotions that would alleviate their plights. The sufferings of Jesus became an occasion of comfort and devotion. This became the spiritual legacy of the fifteenth century:

---

34 For more on Francis, see http://en.wikipedia.org/wiki/Francis_of_Assisi, http://www.biography.com/people/st-francis-of-assisi-21152679, and http://www.newadvent.org/cathen/06221a.htm. Accessed June 1, 2015.

35 Sloyan, *Crucifixion of Jesus,* 136.

36 See http://www.eyewitnesstohistory.com/plague.htm and http://www.historylearningsite.co.uk/black_death_of_1348_to_1350.htm. Accessed June 1, 2015.

This theme [of the extreme painfulness of Christ's suffering] was developed by the authors of meditations, by preachers and artists using texts from both Testaments of the Bible indiscriminately and embellishing as their imagination or devotion dictated. There developed, as a result, devotions to the way of the cross, to Christ tied to the pillar, to the holy face, to the wounds, and to the side of Christ. There even came to be the practice of self-flagellation in imitation of the Crucified.

The cross was the center of it all: the Savior dying on it, his words spoken from it, his deposition from it and entombment. The cross as the sacred emblem of redemption was found everywhere: on buildings sacred and profane, in wayside shrines, in private homes, on one's person. . . . It was as if the Christian populace of Europe was smitten by the new license it was allowing itself and was terrified by the shortness and brutality of life; hence it was determined to make reparation by joining itself to the sufferings of the Savior.[37]

While a detailed history of devotion to the cross and Christ's sufferings, particularly his wounds, is not possible here, suffice it to say that by the end of the Middle Ages, on the eve of the Reformation, Christ's death had become a powerful symbol to which believers were drawn. This entailed several theological consequences. The crucifixion became the sole focus of salvation; Christ's death was narratively severed from the stories of his life and, most important, his resurrection. The brutality of life meant that any hope of union with God in the here and now, any appeal to participation in Christ's glorified life, was forgotten and replaced with a concern for salvation in the hereafter. The believer was taken up with the task of identifying with Christ's suffering now while waiting for a better life, pending God's judgment, in the future. Finally,

[handwritten margin note: By way of theo. of interpretation not nec. actual actual intention]

---

37 Sloyan, *Crucifixion of Jesus*, 138–39. One late medieval figure for whom the passion held particular salience was the anonymous recluse known only as Julian Norwich (d. 1413). She is famous for recording thirteen visions of Christ on the cross that she received, as *Shewings* ("revelations"). See Sloyan's discussion of her, *Crucifixion of Jesus*, 139–40. See also *The Showings of Julian of Norwich*, ed. Denise N. Baker (New York: W. W. Norton, 2004).

Jesus's sufferings themselves were seen to be the effective cause of salvation. Followers endured suffering as a way of doing penance and thus completing the process of their redemption.[38]

We may find this spirituality to be foreign to our current practices, but it is worth noting that this focus on Christ's suffering remains in our hymnody today. Two examples will have to suffice. First, Paul Gerhardt (1607–1676) composed the German hymn "O Haupt voll Blut und Wunden" based on a Latin verse from Bernard of Clairvaux:

O Sacred Head surrounded

By crown of piercing thorn

O bleeding Head, so wounded

Reviled and put to scorn,

Our sins have marred the glory

Of your most holy face,

Yet angel hosts adore thee,

And tremble as they gaze.

(Trans. Henry William Baker)[39]

This was put to music by J. S. Bach and is now a well-beloved hymn sung every year in Holy Week. A verse from the modern version of the hymn is as follows:

What Thou, my Lord, hast suffered, was all for sinners' gain;

Mine, mine was the transgression, but Thine the deadly pain.

Lo, here I fall, my Savior! 'Tis I deserve Thy place;

Look on me with Thy favor, vouchsafe to me Thy grace.[40]

Second, there are the many hymns by Charles Wesley whose influence go well beyond the Methodist movement of his day. The first stanza of a hymn in a 1739 collection remains a favorite today:

And can it be that I should gain

An interest in the Savior's blood?

---

38 For more on the piety of suffering, see Sloyan, *Crucifixion of Christ,* chap. 7, esp. pp. 184–85.

39 Quoted in ibid., 143.

40 See http://cyberhymnal.org/htm/o/s/osacredh.htm. Accessed June 1, 2015.

Died he for me who caused his pain?

For me? Who him to death pursued?

Amazing love, how can it be?

That thou, my God, shouldst die for me?[41]

Thus, the practice of revering the sufferings of Jesus, especially as occurring because of my sin and in my stead, brings the medieval piety forward to our own day.

## Common Sense and Theory

Before moving on to the developments that came with the rise of modern science, let us note two different ways of "making sense" that are illustrated in this chapter. We noted in the previous chapter that the earliest Christians urgently sought to make intelligible their experience of the resurrection and Christ's crucifixion as part of God's plan. In this chapter we have traced something of this ongoing task, as the church leaders dealt with competing interpretations of Christ's work and as the Church moved into the era of Christendom. Christ as victor over the evil deceiver, as well as the new Adam who reestablishes the human race in the image of God, played prominent roles.

All of these attempts were in the realm of common sense. Common sense is the sense-making of a culture, the stories, images, and reasoning that grants a cultural group coherence. Common sense lies in the wisdom of practicality. Its goal is concrete outcomes, in this case lives lived in adherence to the good news that God communicated in the Christ event.

Theory moves beyond things as they appear to us (description) to things as they are in relation to one another (explanation). It usually requires technical language to define terms clearly. It arises from within common sense, when issues emerge that common images and narratives cannot sort out. For example, the terms "hot" and "cold" are descriptive terms, but are not much use when one wants to explain the relationship between degrees of heat in forging different kinds of metal. Likewise, one can wax eloquent about the beauty of a sunset, but "sunset" does not

---

41 Frank Whaling, ed., *John and Charles Wesley: Selected Prayers, Hymns, Journal Notes, Sermons, Letters, and Treatises* (New York: Paulist Press, 1981), 197, as quoted in Sloyan, *Crucifixion of Jesus,* 144.

accurately explain the movement of the earth around the sun. A theory of the solar system is needed, with precise observations that can ground the relations of planets to one another and to the sun, independent of an observer.

In Christian theology, the need for theory arose in the third and fourth centuries with regard to the question of the Son's relation to the Father. Thus, for example, the technical term *homousios* had to be distinguished from *homoiousios*. The Son is of the *same* being (*homo*-ousios) rather than of *similar* being (*homoi*-ousios) to the Father. A series of councils—from Nicea (325) to Chalcedon (451)—were needed to define this relation and then to clarify the relation within the incarnate Son between his human and his divine natures.[42]

Anselm's work in *Cur Deus Homo?* marks a move beyond common sense to theory with regard to an understanding of salvation. He takes for granted what the earlier controversies yielded in terms of the Son's humanity and divinity. The question of Christ's salvific work never became a subject of ecclesiastical definition. Anselm, with his effort to *explain* the need for Christ to become human and die—his appeal to *ratio et necessitas*—serves as a first attempt to be systematic and theoretical about salvation. He found the earlier images to have a certain beauty, but he wanted to move beyond description (salvation as experienced) to explanation (terms and relations in themselves).

Still, this was only a first attempt, and Anselm left many loose ends untied. In addition, there is always a certain tension between theoretical and commonsense discourse, since words in one domain are often confused or misinterpreted in the other domain. It is no surprise, then, that Anselm's careful attempt to explain the logic of God's solution to human sin still requires nuance in order to avoid a commonsense appropriation by which Christ's sufferings came to be seen as the efficient cause of our salvation. Charles Hefling speaks of it as follows:

> But while in Anselm's account the cross is neither unjust nor retributive, he left a few ends untied. Tying

---

42 For more on the first seven councils, see http://en.wikipedia.org/wiki/First_seven_ Ecumenical_Councils. For more on the various positions that were rejected as heresies, see http://en.wikipedia.org/wiki/List_of_Christian_heresies. For more on technical positions within the Christological controversies, see http://en.wikipedia.org/wiki/File:Christology_ Flowchart.PNG. All accessed June 1, 2015.

them, by integrating his new satisfaction theory with the longstanding belief that in giving his life Christ paid some kind of penalty, is a task that has been attempted many times, and this is not the place to rehearse the attempts. Briefly, however, you have only to let the notion of retribution cross the line that Anselm so firmly drew between punishment and satisfaction in order to find yourself headed towards some form of "penal substitution" as the focus of Christ's redeeming work. Whereas for Anselm punishment and retribution go together but have nothing to do with the satisfaction Christ made, they *are* that satisfaction for penal substitution theories. . . . In the theology of penal substitution Good Friday is not so much a case of satisfaction, which means literally "*doing* enough," as of satis*passion*, of Christ's "*suffering* enough" to expiate or make amends for the sins of the world.[43]

The importance of theoretical argument is illustrated here, since making careful distinctions, such as that between satisfaction and retributive punishment, is crucial for authentic religious living. At the same time, we need to acknowledge that lived religion will always carry its power through symbols, narratives, analogies, rituals, devotional practices, and heartfelt commitments. It is not the case that good theoretical argument will take the place of the wisdom that lies in commonsense religious living. We cannot judge the medieval devotions to the wounds of Christ and his suffering to be necessarily inauthentic. We *can* insist that symbolic meaning—the world of metaphors and images—should not be mistaken for theory. We need not ruin the beauty of a lovely sunset by engaging in lectures on the solar system. At the same time, if we insist that because the sunset is beautiful it must be true that the sun orbits the earth, we will have mistaken poetry for theory.

Both good theory and good common sense aim at making the world intelligible and at producing good communities of lives well lived. The former does this through reasoned argument while the latter does it through mentoring and example, capturing hearts and minds with good

---

43 Hefling, "Perhaps Permanently Valid Achievement," 60–61, italics in original. For the theoretical problems that a penal substitution approach must address, see ibid., 61–62.

liturgy, art, drama, music, and playful interaction. While both are subject to the distortions we call sin, to biased argument or political manipulation, the two can serve to correct one another. Grounding concrete practices in an accurate explanation of the world as it works, even the world of God's grace, can set piety on the right course. Likewise, theoretical reasoning is proven adequate when it informs common sense and common living.

# Conclusion

What have we learned that might serve us well in outlining salvation for our contemporary world? What key concepts come to the fore from this *potpourri* of attempts to live and explain God's work in Christ?

Conceptually, the idea that Christ has been victorious over the powers of evil in the world comes to the fore. This victory is nuanced by a rejection of a dualistic worldview in which "spiritual knowledge" saves some—those enlightened by a savior—from the evil of material existence. With Irenaeus we can affirm that the root of evil is the human inclination to usurp for itself divine powers, not material existence itself. Likewise, it is important not to assume that evil—or "the evil one" as iconic of the principalities and powers of this world—is an equal partner in a struggle against God. Any power evil has is a power God has allowed, given his creation of human freedom. With Augustine we need to insist that the victory Christ has won over evil, sin, and death was won not by overpowering evil but through Christ's adherence to his own divine life and its consequences. Loving justice, not power, is God's *modus operandi*.

With Anselm we learn that satisfaction is not punishment. The heart of Christ's work lies in his willing obedience to suffer death, or rather to live a life that would lead to death, even though he did not deserve it. The love at the center of this self-offering, not the death itself or the violence incurred in it, is the key to paying the debt that humankind owes to God because of sin. In all of it—justice not power, satisfaction not punishment, loving self-offering in spite of consequences—Christ serves not only to free us from sin but to provide a model we can imitate.

Finally, while we can be wary of the eccentric if not pathological elements of a focus on Christ's sufferings *as salvific in themselves*, we can recognize the strength of identifying with Christ in his sufferings. Placing ourselves in the drama of his life, death, and resurrection can play a powerful role in transforming our lives and the lives of our communities. Salvation is about covenant love, not contract and reward. The more we enter into relationship with the dying and rising Christ, the more our lives change. The powers of evil are not a phenomenon of the distant past but very present realities in our world. Christ continues to die and rise over and over again. Embracing that story and willingly offering ourselves to it can indeed become part of the ongoing salvation of the world.

# 4

## From Theory to Modernity

### Meaning-Making Today

We have now examined a range of efforts to make sense of what God was doing through Jesus's life, death, and resurrection—from Jesus himself to Paul, the early church fathers, and Anselm. We gave particular attention to Anselm's attempt to give a theoretical account of why Christ's life and death provided a "satisfaction" for human sin, winning the human race exemption from the punishment that God's justice would otherwise have exacted. While Anselm's work represents a rudimentary move to theory, it nonetheless has had a powerful influence over the last one thousand years of theologizing.[1] At the same time, the strength of symbolic meaning, particularly when it comes to participating in Christ's suffering, is evident in popular devotional practices that emerged in the Middle Ages and carry great iconic power today. While this symbolic

---

1 For more on developments of the medieval concept of satisfaction, see Patout Burns, "The Concept of Satisfaction in Medieval Redemption Theory," *Theological Studies* 36 (1975): 285–304.

meaning continues to serve an important role in believers' lives, it is easy to see how the careful nuance of "either satisfaction or punishment" can be lost and Christ's suffering in itself can come to be seen as salvific.

This chapter will continue in an historical vein. The objective, however, is not to provide a survey of further theological personages and their understandings of salvation.[2] Rather, we are here concerned with our modern world and the ways in which our questions about faith are radically different than they were in the worlds of Paul, the church fathers, Anselm, or believers in the Middle Ages. This issue is that of "modernity," or what some would now call "postmodernity." Our focus is on the last five hundred years, specifically the rise of modern science and a new sense of history, and how their advent has radically changed the assumptions we make about ourselves, about the world around us, and about the role of religion in that world.

# The Renaissance and the Rise of Modern Science

One of the hallmarks of our modern culture is a celebration of the power of the human mind, and the ability of everyone to think for himself or herself. To trace the emergence of this emphasis, we will go back to the late Middle Ages and the Italian Renaissance.[3] In contrast to the decline of life in Europe in the fourteenth century, a group of Italian thinkers in the late 1300s declared that the era of the barbarous Middle Ages was over. A new "rebirth" was coming about. This *renaissance,* as it came to be known, hearkened back to the ideals of Greece and Rome. It rejoiced in all things human—the wonders of the human body, the unlimited reach of the human mind, and the grandeur of human rhetoric. These ancient ideals were brought forward and heralded over against what was taken to be the stifling obedience expected by the Catholic Church.

---

2 For a survey of this kind, see David A. Brondos, *Fortress Introduction to Salvation and the Cross* (Minneapolis: Fortress Press, 2007); William P. Loewe, *Lex Crucis: Soteriology and the Stages of Meaning* (Minneapolis: Fortress Press, 2016); L. W. Grensted, *A Short History of the Doctrine of the Atonement* (London: Longmans, Green and Co., 1920).

3 See http://www.learner.org/interactives/renaissance/index.html. Accessed May 26, 2015.

This rebirth had its start in Italy for several reasons. In the fifteenth century Italy was made up of independent city-states. These included the papal states (around Rome), Venice, and Milan. Prominent among these was the city of Florence, where the wealthy Medici family flaunted their money by becoming patrons of the arts and intellectual life. This patronage allowed scholars and artists to visit the ruins of ancient Greece and Rome that were scattered across the Italian peninsula. In addition, the 1453 fall of Constantinople (Istanbul, Turkey today) to the Ottoman Empire meant the end of the Byzantine Roman Empire and, effectively, the end of Christendom in the East.[4] This led to a steady stream of Greek Christian scholars fleeing into Italy, bringing their language and their artifacts, particularly Greek texts, with them. Among other things, these texts included manuscripts of the New Testament in the original Greek, leading eventually to published editions of the New Testament in Greek. New translations of this Greek New Testament into vernacular languages played an important role in the Protestant Reformation.

The Italian Renaissance is associated with the rise of a new philosophy—humanism. "Humanism" coins a term that captures the focus of this new perspective, which spread from Italy northward in the fourteenth and fifteenth centuries.[5] While not explicitly anti-Christian, it celebrated a freedom of thought not hampered by church authorities. The power of wonder and the appreciation of beauty came to the fore. People were encouraged to be curious and to question received wisdom.[6] Experimentation and observation were highlighted. So it is that one of the great artists of the era, Leonardo da Vinci, not only painted but also studied human anatomy by dissecting corpses, and undertook the design of a flying machine.

Among the technological advances that came in the fifteenth century, one stands out as changing the course of history. This is the invention of the printing press, with movable type, by the German Johannes Gutenberg in 1445.[7] Previously, books had to be copied by hand on

---

4  See http://wikipedia.org/wiki/Fall_of_Constantinople. Accessed May 26, 2015.

5  See "humanism" in *Encyclopaedia Britannica Online Academic Edition*, Encyclopædia Britannica Inc., 2014, http://www.britannica.com/EBchecked/topic/275932/humanism. Accessed May 26, 2015.

6  Note that the Renaissance and the humanism that accompanied it mostly affected a cultural elite. Life of the ordinary citizen was little affected by these movements.

7  See http://www.biography.com/people/johannes-gutenberg-9323828. Accessed May 26, 2015.

to parchments made from animal skins. The printing press meant that multiple copies of a single text could be made quickly and cheaply. The movable type meant that one could switch from one text to a new text fairly easily, producing many different books in short order. It also cut down on the errors that would be made when texts were copied by hand. New ways of manufacturing paper assisted in the rapid advance of book publication.

The impact of the printing press cannot be overstated. In an era when human wonder was celebrated, and new manuscripts were being discovered from ancient cultures, it created a revolution in knowledge. A growing middle class living in urban settings fostered a new market for mass-produced books. Whereas earlier texts had been in classical languages such as Latin (including the Vulgate translation of the Bible, which had dominated scholarship and church lectionaries for over one thousand years), these new readers were demanding books in their vernacular languages. This included new translations of the Bible. The availability of such books meant a growing literacy; whereas previously only elites with leisure time were able to read, now the ordinary citizen was eager to read as well. The new ideas of the Renaissance in the fifteenth century and the Protestant Reformation in the sixteenth century were able to spread quickly and cheaply.

While the Protestant Reformation was indeed fueled by religious issues, the actions of Martin Luther (1483–1546) serve to illustrate the revolutionary effects of the Renaissance, humanism, and the printing press on sixteenth-century Europe. On October 31, 1517, as legend has it, Martin Luther posted his Ninety-Five Theses on the Wittenberg University chapel door, protesting the sale of indulgences by the Catholic Church.[8] He wrote them in Latin, expecting a scholarly dialogue to ensue. But due to the printing press, these were copied and distributed throughout Germany within two weeks and throughout Europe within two months. What had started as an internal ecclesial dispute soon grew to have popular dimensions. Furthermore, when Luther was condemned by the emperor with the pope's blessing, Luther went to hide in Wartburg Castle for an extended period of time. There he undertook the translation

---

8  This action on Luther's part would have been the sixteenth-century equivalent of tweeting or posting something on a blog today. It was a public action meant to start a discussion. On indulgences, see http://www.britannica.com/EBchecked/topic/286800/indulgence. Accessed May 26, 2015.

of the Bible into German, thus providing the German populace with a text they could read and understand.

Another figure who fueled a revolution of a different kind was Nicolaus Copernicus (1473–1543). Born of a wealthy family in Torun, Poland, Copernicus spent his life as a canon at the Cathedral of Frombork in Poland, a position arranged by his uncle, the bishop of Varmia. While this position demanded much of his time and attention, it also allowed him some leisure to pursue his interests in astronomy. His observations of the night sky, combined with some mathematical calculations, brought him to challenge the long-held view of the cosmos propagated by Ptolemy in the second century CE and accepted by church authorities for centuries. Ptolemy's view was *geocentric*, assuming the earth was the center of the universe. Copernicus suggested, in contrast, that the earth and other planets revolved around the sun—a *heliocentric* view of the cosmos. While Copernicus was not the first to make such a suggestion—a Greek astronomer named Aristarchus had advocated such a view several centuries before Christ—he was the first to combine observation, theory, and mathematical calculations in order to "prove" his theory.[9]

So the Copernican Revolution was twofold. On the one hand, the publication of *De revolutionibus orbium coelestium* (On the Revolution of the Heavenly Spheres) just before Copernicus's death in 1543 met with church condemnation and popular skepticism. Martin Luther dismissed it and, in spite of the fact that it was dedicated to Pope Paul III, it was eventually banned by the Catholic Church. The idea that the earth was not at the center of the cosmos simply upset too much that was culturally and religiously taken for granted. Theologically, it challenged the idea that earth was the apex of God's creative work. Further, there was an entire social order tied up in the geocentric view, including a hierarchy of knowledge and of governance. When Luther's assistant, Andreas Osiander, dismissed Copernicus's work by saying, "This fool wants to turn the whole art of astronomy upside down,"[10] it was not only astronomy that was being "turned upside down."

The second aspect of this revolution was just as threatening. This

---

9 For more on Copernicus and his contributions to science, see "Nicolaus Copernicus," *The Biography Channel*, http://www.biography.com/people/nicolaus-copernicus-9256984. Accessed May 26, 2015.

10 Ibid.

was a revolution in how we go about discovering the world around us. Copernicus, and many who followed him, based their theories on observation and calculation. This, of course, we now take for granted. But in the fifteenth and sixteenth centuries this was novel. The Aristotelian approach to understanding the world began with philosophy. The starting point was *metaphysics,* or the study of the nature of reality itself, the nature of *being.* What we consider science today was a subdivision of this philosophical quest. So, for example, biology involved explaining the nature of being when beings are *alive.* While noticing phenomena in the world played a part, the primary tools were logic and *endoxa,* or considered opinion. Arguments from logic had to do with what made sense in a consistent manner. If one took a position, or defended a truth, but was sloppy or inconsistent in one's reasoning, one's position could be dismissed. Appeal to recognized authorities was a matter of respect. How long has an idea been around and who has subscribed to it in the past? Are these views those of reputable judges? So, for example, when Thomas Aquinas adopted this method in his *Summa Theologiae,* he appealed to Augustine, or Paul, or other scriptural texts, and the Philosopher (meaning Aristotle himself) to support his positions.[11]

Copernicus did not set out to change any of this. But by default he began a different trend. By defending his position based on many hours of charting the night skies, combined with an effort to systematize what he was seeing in a mathematically coherent way, he began what we now take for granted in our scientific methods. But in the process he shifted the starting point of inquiry, from philosophical or theological first premises to empirical observation. Likewise he changed the grounds on which an explanation is judged to be correct. Rather than logic and esteemed opinion, the criteria of judgment became mathematical calculation and documented observations.

Galileo Galilei (1564–1642) was born two decades after Copernicus died but he stands within the legacy that Copernicus left, not only because he defended Copernicus's ideas but because he adopted his methods. He made pioneering observations that grounded new

---

11 For more on Aristotle and science, see Christopher Shields, "Aristotle," *The Stanford Encyclopedia of Philosophy* (Spring 2014 Edition), Edward N. Zalta (ed.), at http://plato. stanford.edu/archives/spr2014/entries/aristotle/, and Andrea Falcon, "Aristotle on Causality," *The Stanford Encyclopedia of Philosophy* (Spring 2014 Edition), Edward N. Zalta (ed.), at http://plato.stanford.edu/archives/spr2014/entries/aristotle-causality/ . Both accessed May 26, 2015.

understandings of physics which survive to this day. For example, he observed the swinging of a pendulum from a Cathedral ceiling and, by timing its gradual winding down, established that the *arc* of a pendulum does not change the time it takes to wind down. However, the *length* of the pendulum does make a difference. These basic observations and conclusions set the stage for the development of the modern clock. Likewise, Galileo is most famous for testing Aristotle's claim that heavier objects fall faster than lighter ones. By conducting experiments dropping objects off a tower in Pisa, his hometown, he showed that objects of different weights fall at the same rate.

One of Galileo's most important contributions to modern science was his invention of the telescope, in fact a series of ever more effective telescopes. This allowed him to gather more and better observations about the heavens, including the discovery that the moon is not smooth but pock-marked with gullies, and that Jupiter has a number of its own moons. Galileo's observations led him to affirm the heliocentric position of Copernicus. His defense of Copernicus got him into controversy with the religious authorities of his day. He spent the last years of his life under house arrest.[12] While the drama of Galileo and his relationship with the Catholic Church is fascinating, the important point here is that he, too, shifted the way in which intellectual claims were reached and defended. Observation and calculation were his methods. What was so revolutionary was the fact that these methods did not require endorsing theological or philosophical positions nor appealing to agents of knowledge such as scholars or church officials.

Thus, Copernicus and Galileo ushered in a cultural revolution that continues even to today. They themselves did not realize the impact of their new methods but they were, de facto, asserting that knowledge did not come from logical argument or learned reputation alone but also from the operations of the human mind observing the world around it. In effect this meant that one's position in society did not establish the validity of one's knowledge. One might hold a particular ecclesial office or hold a chair at a university but this did not mean that one's views were necessarily correct. Instead, anyone could make observations for

---

12 For more on Galileo, see "Galileo," *The Biography Channel website,* http://www. biography.com/people/galileo-9305220. Accessed May 26, 2015. See also David Sobel, *Galileo's Daughter: A Historical Memoir of Science, Faith, and Love* (New York: Penguin Books, 2000).

themselves, could be a judge of truth. Even further, it seemed that setting aside theological claims was a requisite for unbiased observation.

Herbert Butterfield, in *The Origins of Modern Science, 1300–1800*, sets the year 1680 as the point at which modern science had become culturally established.[13] It was by this time that the common populace began to accept this new approach to truth and authority. Its implications were yet to be worked out. But Butterfield claims that this scientific revolution "outshines everything since the rise of Christianity and reduces the Renaissance and the Reformation to the rank of mere episodes, mere internal displacements, within the system of medieval Christendom."[14]

## Impact and Implications

This was a revolution not just in *what* we know about the material world but in our grasp of *how* we know it. It developed into what we can call the *discovery of discovery*. It is not that previously people knew things in a different way; it was our understanding *of understanding* that gradually shifted. Truth is not merely what is handed down from on high but something that can be unearthed from below upward, so to speak. One makes observations, sets out hypotheses, then verifies these with further observations. The better tools one has for gathering data (such as telescopes or microscopes), the more accurate one's observations and the more precise one's theories. Further questions can be raised, leading to refinement of the facts. This is the heart of modern scientific method, and no matter how sophisticated our enquiries become, they cycle through these tasks over and over again. While a full articulation of this process of discovery was not immediately forthcoming in the late seventeenth century, it was this new way of proving theories through empirical verification that, in practice, engendered a cultural revolution.

It is no surprise, then, that just as Herbert Butterfield marks 1680 as the beginning of modern science, so also Paul Hazard sets 1680 as

---

13 Herbert Butterfield, *The Origins of Modern Science, 1300–1800*, 2nd ed. (New York: Free Press, 1966). This is discussed in Bernard J. F. Lonergan, "Theology in Its New Context," in *Second Collection*, ed. William F. J. Ryan and Bernard J. Tyrrell (London: Darton, Longman, and Todd, 1974), 55.

14 Butterfield, *Origins*, vii.

the start of the Enlightenment.[15] This was an era known as the Age of Reason, in which the powers of the human mind were celebrated throughout the Western world. There was great optimism about the reach of human capacities; no question was too big to be asked nor too complex to be answered, given the requisite time and resources. The new tools of modern science were expected to solve many of humankind's greatest dilemmas. It was also a period that highlighted the autonomy of individual thinking. Immanuel Kant (1724–1804), in answering the question "What is Enlightenment?" coined the phrase *Sapere Aude!*—"Dare to know!"[16] The French philosopher Voltaire (1694–1778)—a skeptic and critic of religious fideism—declared, "Dare to think for yourself."[17] Indeed, the American Declaration of Independence (1776) reflects this defense of autonomy and the rights of individual conscience.

This great confidence in human reason had its impact on religion and its place in the social milieu. Paul Hazard insists that between 1680 and 1715 there was already a full flung attack against Christianity from all directions. Perpetual religious wars had recurred in the century after the Reformation, and this bloodshed was regarded as evidence of the negative impact of religious faith. The God of Christianity was replaced by the God of the philosophers, such as Voltaire and Kant. In time, even this philosophical bent was replaced with agnosticism and atheism.[18]

Isaac Newton (1642–1717) was born the year that Galileo died. He became the father of modern physics, inventing a new mathematics—calculus—and defining the law of gravity. He illustrates the bridge between traditional Christian faith and the abandonment of faith altogether by scientists that followed. He himself wrote as much about theology as he did about science, but his faith was unorthodox.[19] Among other things he asserted that, if in an endeavor to explain scientific processes we come upon some element that seems inexplicable, we can appeal to God as a causal agent. For example, his calculations about planetary orbits did

---

15 Paul Hazard, *The European Mind: 1680–1715* (London: Hollis and Carter, 1953).

16 Immanuel Kant, *Foundations of the Metaphysics of Morals* and *What Is Enlightenment?* trans. L. W. Beck (New York: Liberal Arts Press, 1959), 85.

17 See http://www.panarchy.org/voltaire/thought.html. Accessed May 26, 2015.

18 See discussion of this in Lonergan, "Theology," 57. See also Michael J. Buckley, *At the Origins of Modern Atheism* (New Haven, CT: Yale University Press, 1987).

19 Newton's beliefs were non-Trinitarian. See Stephen Snobelen, "Isaac Newton, Heretic: The Strategies of a Nicodemite," *British Journal for the History of Science* 32 (1999): 381–419.

not come out quite right; his theory of gravity could not explain why the planets did not collapse on one another. He felt free in this case to appeal to God as intervening in order to ensure the stability of the solar system. This view came to be seen as the "God of the gaps" strategy; explain phenomena as well as you can by scientific means, then appeal to God as a causal agent to make it all come out right.[20]

This combination of science and appeals to God satisfied a certain generation of Enlightenment scientists. But the more that science advanced in its ability to correct errors and refine previous achievements, the less it needed to appeal to divine interventions. Pierre-Simon Laplace (1749–1827) represents the science that emerged two generations after Newton. With more refined mathematical processes, he was able to make advances in establishing what kept the solar system stable. The story is that when he presented his new book to Napoleon Bonaparte, who was something of an amateur mathematician himself, Napoleon commented that there was no discussion of God in the book. To this, Laplace is said to have replied, "I have no need of that hypothesis."

Thus the separation of science and religion was complete. Modern science depended on empirical observation and verification, combined with mathematical calculation and theoretical analysis. None of this required belief in a divine being. In fact, given the state of religious affairs at the time, ignoring religious doctrines, or at least setting them aside, seemed necessary for the advancement of knowledge. The initial revolution that turned to empirical observation had developed into a view that insisted that only knowledge garnered from empirical observation was valid. This "empiricism" ignored any truth claims that couldn't be "seen," thus dismissing theological perspectives altogether.

If anything, one could appeal to the god of deism—a generic faith in a Creator who established world order in the beginning but then let it go on its own way. This God rewards good and punishes evil, but in a general way; there is justice immanent in the order of the universe. This God does not intervene nor does he have intimate relationships with believers. Jesus was a good example but is not a current presence. This generic faith solved many problems culturally. It allowed for a public religion; indeed it is at the heart of the American experiment. At the

---

20 See Cynthia Crysdale and Neil Ormerod, *Creator God, Evolving World* (Minneapolis: Fortress Press, 2013), 4–5.

same time it freed social life from parochial bloodshed. So freedom of religion became a hallmark of the U.S. Constitution. Benjamin Franklin and Thomas Jefferson were deists—religious men who disavowed allegiance to any one religious institution or set of doctrines.

So by the end of the eighteenth century there was a growing divide between science and religion. The scientific endeavor dealt with hard facts that could be proven empirically, without any need for appeals to the divine. While science dealt with such facts, religion had to do with mere opinion, with matters that were simply believed and could not be proven. Reason was hailed as something all could appeal to, while faith was a personal set of convictions. Hence, the public/private divide emerged. Science and reasoned argument were in the public domain. Beyond the realm of a publically acceptable deism, religious beliefs and practices were private affairs. One could light candles, say prayers, genuflect or baptize, celebrate Passover or sit shiva, but all in the privacy of one's own home or religious institution.

We will examine the response of the religious establishment to this rise of empirical method in due course. But first we need to highlight one other effect of this discovery of discovery. Recall that one of the main features that emerged was the notion that just about anyone could become a knower and learner. If knowledge is not something handed down from those "in the know," then anyone in the street could consider himself an agent of discovery. If truth comes from observation and experimentation, in theory anyone who could use his or her five senses could become a judge of true or false claims. Thus the *discovery of discovery* led to the *democratization of knowledge.* It was not that every citizen became an expert in all fields, but that each person could consider himself or herself an agent of knowing; in theory he or she *could* become an expert, regardless of social status. This, combined with growing literacy in all social classes and the increasing availability of books, led, literally, to revolutionary action.

If we date the beginning of the Enlightenment and the rise of modern science at 1680, it is no surprise that two political revolutions would take place a century later. The American Revolution began with the Declaration of Independence in 1776.[21] The French Revolution took

---

21 See "American Revolution History" on *The History Channel website,* http://www.history. com/topics/american-revolution/american-revolution-history. Accessed May 26, 2015.

place in 1789.[22] In both cases, the authority of monarchs and the aristocracy was challenged. The American slogan "no taxation without repre-
sentation" signified the belief in popular sovereignty and the assumption
that the ordinary citizen should have a say in government policies. The
French Revolution led to great bloodshed when the peasants demanded
to have a say in political life and executed the powers that be. In both
cases, had there not been a previous revolution in understanding discovery and its methods, it is unlikely that the political revolutions would
have taken place. The hallmark of the emerging democracies—the claim
to unalienable rights of all citizens—had its ground in the democratization of knowledge fostered by a new understanding of understanding.[23]

## The Churches' Response

What, then, of the religious establishment? How did it react to this new
world of empirical science? The rejection of the heliocentric views of
Copernicus and Galileo by church authorities is well documented. But
just as the Copernican Revolution was about much more than the solar
system, so both the Protestant churches and the Roman Catholic establishment did not look kindly on the challenges that arose with regard to
truth and authority.

Recall that at the center of the revolutionary *discovery of discovery*
was the dismissal of authorities as sources of truth. Truths were proven
through empirical means and only that which was so proven was real.
The realm of religion was dismissed as ephemeral and the approval of
religious authorities was forgotten if not downright eliminated. Church
authorities were threatened, to say the least. Not only was their social
role as experts on matters of both faith and scholarship being challenged,
more importantly the very ground of divine *revelation* was at stake.

The church had always held that God's ways are not man's ways,

---

22 See "The French Revolution" on *The History Channel website,* http://www.history.com/
    topics/french-revolution. Accessed May 26, 2015.

23 Note that these newfound rights, and the democratization of knowledge, applied initially to
    only a subset of the relevant populations: propertied white males. In the American context,
    it took another two hundred years for the implications of this cultural turn to human
    agency to actually apply to all—women, African Americans, and Native Americans. For a
    humorous rendition of this limitation, see http://mrcozart.wordpress.com/2013/01/18/equal-
    rights-french-revolution-grade-9/. Accessed May 26, 2015.

and that throughout history God had revealed himself in special ways to particular people at particular times and places. Most notably, of course, was the revelation that came through the incarnation of Jesus Christ. In what came to be the Protestant traditions, this set of revealed truths is enshrined in the Holy Scriptures, as heralded in Luther's insistence on *sola scriptura*; only Scripture is authoritative for faith. In the Roman Catholic world, as defended at the Council of Trent (1545–1547; 1559–1563), divine revelation is embedded in the tradition of the church; the church is the locus of revelation and therefore the bearer of truth.

The issues of authority and truth came to a head in the nineteenth century for both groups, in different ways. Though not articulated as such, the questions were "How do we come to know truth?" and "To whom are these truths entrusted?" The dramas by which these questions were addressed unfolded in the 1800s, though the topics debated in Protestant circles varied from those in the Roman Catholic domain.

In Protestant circles, by the early nineteenth century, new methods of biblical interpretation were being used. Parallel to Galileo and modern scientists, attention to observation became the starting point for understanding the meaning of the Bible. In this case, however, one was "observing" a text or set of texts. Such observation meant approaching a text without any preconceived theological ideas. Rather than try to draw a consistent set of meanings out of the variety of books that made up the Bible, the idea was to let each book speak for itself, in the context in which it was written.

This idea was a subset of emerging literary and historical criticism. The methods of "hard" science were adapted to apply to the human science of understanding historical texts. Why not treat the book of Mark, for example, just like one would treat ancient Greek tragedies or William Shakespeare's *Hamlet*? To grasp the meanings involved, one needed to explore the historical context and the specified audience for which a text was written. Just as modern science relied on setting aside traditional views in order to generate truth, so these biblical interpreters set aside theological positions in order to historically situate Mark, or Paul, or the letter to the Hebrews. What resulted was a recognition that these authors had different contextual realities and generated diverse theologies to meet the needs of their audiences.

Needless to say, such endeavors put the entire enterprise of determining theological truth into a tailspin. The new methods of biblical analysis did not require adherence to the Christian faith at all. In fact, they presumed that greater objectivity was the fruit of critical thinking alone, leaving personal religious commitments to the side. The result, to church adherents, appeared to take all theological truth out of the texts. Scripture as a source of revealed knowledge about God was rejected in favor of a purely human set of interpretations.

One response to this "modernism" is illustrated in the American context by the Niagara Bible Conference. This was actually a series of Bible conferences that met in Niagara Falls, New York, beginning in 1875. This summer resort meeting became the model for many such Bible conferences around the United States in the late 1800s. They consisted of two weeks of preaching and teaching in an effort to defend the "fundamentals" of the faith over against the perceived apostasy of the established churches. The Niagara Conference of 1878 generated a list of fourteen fundamentals essential to true Christian faith, the first of which was biblical inerrancy. In 1910 the General Assembly of the Northern Presbyterian Church took the longer list and affirmed a list of five. These five fundamentals of orthodox Christian belief were (1) the inerrancy of Scripture, (2) the virgin birth of Christ, (3) the substitutionary atonement of Christ, (4) the resurrection of Christ, and (5) the miracle working power of Christ.[24]

These same general issues were at the center of nineteenth-century Roman Catholicism. In 1864 Pope Pius IX published the *Syllabus of Errors*, listing a series of propositions considered to be erroneous. These propositions included the idea that philosophy can be carried on without regard to supernatural revelation. It condemns the idea that reason alone can be the source and test of knowledge, the modern emphasis on autonomy of intellect and choice, and appeals to natural forces as providing a full account of all aspects of reality.[25] In 1869–1870 the pope convoked the First Vatican Council. This council ended prematurely due to the invasion of Rome by forces from the Kingdom of Italy, but before it closed, it published the decree *Pastor Aeternus*. "The decree states that the true successor of St. Peter has full and supreme power of jurisdiction

---

24 For more on fundamentalism, see http://en.wikipedia.org/wiki/Christian_fundamentalism. Accessed May 26, 2015.

25 See http://www.papalencyclicals.net/Pius09/p9syll.htm. Accessed May 26, 2015.

over the whole church; that he has the right of free communication with the pastors of the whole church and with their flocks; and that his primacy includes the supreme teaching power to which Jesus Christ added the prerogative of papal infallibility, whereby the pope is preserved free from error when he teaches definitively that a doctrine concerning faith or morals is to be believed by the whole church."[26]

The importance of this is not the particulars of papal infallibility as much as it is the perceived need to take a position on the truth of revelation and the locus of this revelation in the church. While the center of this debate for Protestants was the validity of the revealed truths in Scripture, for Catholics the questions surfaced around the validity of church authority. In many ways they were the same issues, with differing foci.

After the First Vatican Council, Roman Catholic authorities labeled and condemned Modernism, a movement within the church that accepted new approaches to theology and biblical interpretation. The Encyclopedia Britannica explains this as "a movement in the last decade of the 19th century and first decade of the 20th that sought to reinterpret traditional Catholic teaching in the light of 19th-century philosophical, historical, and psychological theories and called for freedom of conscience. Influenced by non-Catholic biblical scholars, Modernists contended that the writers of both the Old and the New Testaments were conditioned by the times in which they lived and that there had been an evolution in the history of biblical religion."[27] To counteract this tendency, Pope Leo XIII established the Pontifical Biblical Commission in 1903 to monitor the work of Catholic biblical scholars. In 1907 Pope Pius X published the papal encyclical *Pascendi Dominici Gregis*, specifically condemning Modernism.[28] From 1910 onward until the 1960s, all clerics had to take an oath against Modernism before their ordination.

---

26 "First Vatican Council," in *Encyclopaedia Britannica Online Academic Edition*, Encyclopædia Britannica Inc., 2014, http://www.britannica.com/EBchecked/topic/624002/First-Vatican-Council. Accessed May 26, 2015.

27 "Modernism," in *Encyclopaedia Britannica Online Academic Edition*, Encyclopædia Britannica Inc., 201,. http://www.britannica.com/EBchecked/topic/387278/Modernism. Accessed May 26, 2015. See also Anthony Carroll, "Modernism: The Philosophical Foundations" at http://www.thinkingfaith.org/articles/20090724_1.htm. Accessed May 26, 2015.

28 The full encyclical is available at http://www.papalencyclicals.net/Pius10/p10pasce.htm. Accessed May 26, 2015.

Much has happened in Christian circles since the rejection of Modernism and the assertion of fundamentalism. Most important for Roman Catholics was the Second Vatican Council called by Pope John XXIII and held over four years, 1962–1965. John XXIII called for an *aggiornamento*—a "bringing up to date"—and urged the bishops to welcome the advances of the modern world. Likewise, most Protestant scholars now take the higher critical methods of biblical scholarship for granted, and preachers enjoy the fruits of form criticism, source criticism, and historical research as they prepare their sermons. Nevertheless, at the heart of any rapprochement between modern scholarship and theological convictions is the integration of critical historical inquiry and revelation as sources for theology.

# The Turn to the Subject: From Theory to Interiority

Alongside the advances in modern science and critical historical scholarship lay a fundamental shift in philosophy. As we have seen, the new methods highlighted issues of how truths are defined and defended. In fact, the question of how and whether we can know *anything* came to the fore. While religious believers went on the defensive against the hard facts of science and new approaches to history and the Bible, philosophers turned their attention to the knowers themselves. Just what is it that goes on inside the mind when one comes to affirm a given proposition or worldview as correct? More radically, can we ever actually know anything to be true, or is all inquiry merely a matter of what *seems* to be the case—leaving a radical ambiguity about what *really* is the case?

Prior to the shifts of the seventeenth and eighteenth centuries, the focus of philosophers in general was on questions about the nature of *reality*. This is the field of *metaphysics*—can we find basic principles or fundamental elements that make up all of reality, regardless of any particular manifestation of it? Categories such as *potency, form,* and *act*, to borrow from Aquinas (who borrowed from Aristotle), were elements of this metaphysical quest. After the Copernican Revolution and the advent of modern science, philosophical questions shifted from the nature of reality to the nature of *mind*. Philosophers were now concerned, not with metaphysics, but with *epistemology*, the question of knowing.

This "turn to the subject" sets the basic question for all forms of modern philosophy, with inevitable consequences for theology. René Descartes (1596–1650) stands as the earliest representative of this turn. He is famous for his statement *Cogito ergo sum* (I think therefore I am). He endorsed a modern dualism, in this case not between matter and spirit, but between the inner, thinking self, and the material world of extension beyond ourselves—the "objective" world. What we can be most certain of is our internal introspective knowledge and our thoughts as self-conscious.[29] Immanuel Kant (1724–1804) pressed the issues further to ask about "the conditions of the possibility of knowledge." What kinds of conditions would need to be fulfilled if we are to know anything? He postulates that there are *a priori* structures built into the human mind, by which the empirical world of the senses can be known. "Reason itself is structured with forms of experience and categories that give a phenomenal and logical structure to any possible object of empirical experience. These categories cannot be circumvented to get at a mind-independent world, but they are necessary for experience of spatio-temporal objects with their causal behavior and logical properties. These two theses constitute Kant's famous transcendental idealism and empirical realism."[30]

Kant and Descartes illustrate this turn to the subject within philosophical speculation in the seventeenth and eighteenth centuries.[31] But they signal the more general recognition that there is a knowing and acting agent behind all claims about the world, as alluded to above with regard to the rise of modern democracies and the new view of historical agency. In the nineteenth century Sigmund Freud spent a lifetime examining the human subject as a psychological phenomenon. William James turned to religious experience and sought to explain what happens to the person involved in such experiences.[32] The global reach of exploration led to the field of anthropology, in which experts analyzed human arrangements in cultures foreign to the Anglo-European mold. Historians

---

29 His major publication was *Meditations on First Philosophy,* published in 1641. For more, see "Rene Descartes (1596–1650)" in *Internet Encyclopedia of Philosophy,* http://www. iep.utm.edu/descarte/#SH1la. Accessed May 26, 2015.

30 "Immanuel Kant: Metaphysics," in *Internet Encyclopedia of Philosophy,* http://www.iep. utm.edu/kantmeta/. Accessed May 26, 2015.

31 For a website on Kant, see http://people.bu.edu/wwildman/WeirdWildWeb/courses/wphil/ lectures/wphil_theme15.htm. Accessed Feb. 19,, 2016.

32 See the article on William James by Wayne Pomerleau in the *Internet Encyclopedia of Philosophy*—http://www.iep.utm.edu/james-o/. Accessed May 26, 2015.

such as Marx treated history as a drama in which actors played various parts according to their "interests." The discovery of discovery that was implicit in Copernicus and Galileo has led to an explicit interest in and analysis of the "discoverers." The world of "interiority" is now differentiated from both commonsense meanings and systematic theoretical discourse. Now the question is: Just who is this subject—the knower and actor—who understands and makes history?

In the last chapter we discussed the move in Christian theology from common sense to theory. Questions over Christ's humanity and divinity and the nature of the Trinity required such a shift in the third and fourth centuries. Anselm represents an attempt to move beyond description to theoretical explanation with regard to Christ's saving work. This theoretical mode of theologizing then carried the scholarly tradition through the Middle Ages, though of course it never replaced the need for commonsense intelligibility. With this discovery of discoverers, a new exigence arises—the need to take into account the knowers, doers, and experiencers themselves. To use a previous analogy: if the shift from common sense to theory is illustrated by the difference between describing a beautiful sunset and explaining the solar system, the shift from theory to interiority initiates attention to the person watching the sunset. Whereas both in a commonsense mode and in theoretical practice the person experiencing the sunset or trying to understand the solar system remains invisible, this new era invokes a further differentiation of awareness. No longer can the subject doing the watching or the understanding be taken for granted. Instead, scholarly and cultural common sense is now preoccupied with the subject herself.

## Historical Consciousness

One final and pervasive element of contemporary culture requires more elaboration. Recall the explanation of Modernism quoted above: "Modernists contended that the writers of both the Old and the New Testaments were conditioned by the times in which they lived and that there had been an evolution in the history of biblical religion."[33] This notion of an "evolution in history" was at the heart of the rise of historical

---

33 "Modernism," in *Encyclopaedia Britannica Online Academic Edition*, Encyclopædia Britannica Inc., 2014, http://www.britannica.com/EBchecked/topic/387278/Modernism. Accessed May 26, 2015.

consciousness in the nineteenth century, a consciousness that continues to influence our worldviews today.

Several sources led to this new understanding of history and change. Modern science itself demonstrated that ideas about the world around us change from one generation to another. Galileo revised the views of Copernicus. Newton took their basic insights to new horizons, yet Laplace revised Newton further. While modern scientific methods relied on rigorous appeal to observations and "hard facts," they also incorporated the need to ever confirm and/or revise accepted views. Rather than a neat and stable metaphysical system, the result was a series of enterprises that were themselves emerging from one era to the next.

Furthermore, recall the political revolutions at the end of the eighteenth century. The French Revolution in 1789 was followed by a series of revolutions in France over the next hundred years. While the American Revolution led to the establishment of a new country, it involved the defeat of the British Empire in a way that disrupted a national identity. The United States was considered a modern "experiment" and faced many challenges in the nineteenth century, including the War of 1812 against the British and its own Civil War from 1861 to 1865. In essence, what emerged was the common experience that the future could no longer be counted on as a mere extension of the past. Rather, history came to be seen as a series of ruptures in which "normality" had to be created and recreated anew. There was a "constant iteration of the new."[34] Disenchantment with the past came to be a hallmark of modern experience.

Incorporated into this new view of history was the idea that we are no longer passive recipients of what others do. Rather, we—even the peasants—are responsible for what we make of our worlds. We can choose a government, we can overthrow an empire, we can make history what it is. The past is no longer predictive of the future and the actors that make the difference are not the powers that be but each and every person in the street.

At the same time, the idea that the created world itself is shifting and changing was gaining ground. The field of geological science emerged

---

34 See the lecture by Peter Fritzsche, "The Melancholy of History: The Rise of Historical Consciousness in the Nineteenth Century," at http://vimeo.com/63325565. Accessed May 26, 2015.

in the seventeenth century when Christians realized that the Bible itself had different schemes for determining the age of the earth. As this science developed into the nineteenth century, the empirical study of geological forms, especially fossils, led to ever lengthening timeframes for the earth's existence. Charles Lyell (1797–1875) wrote his multivolume *Principles of Geology* (1830–1833), establishing that the earth itself was a series of disruptions and was in an ever-constant state of change. This was confirmed as major expeditions circumnavigated the world, bringing back to Europe multiple artifacts indicating an ever-widening world of present and past flora and fauna.[35]

One such expedition, that of the *Beagle* (1831–1835), included Charles Darwin as naturalist. His observations and his collections of animal specimens both confirmed Lyell's theories and led to Darwin's own theory of biological "descent by modification." After years of delaying publication due to his fear of the reaction it would garner, in 1859 Darwin published *On the Origin of Species by Means of Natural Selection*.[36] With this set of ideas, and the controversy it stirred up, the whole question of historical stability versus constant change came to be front and center in the public eye.

Like the Copernican Revolution, while the issues discussed were often about specific biblical texts, the truly disturbing factors lay at a deeper level. Not only did Darwin displace humans from the center of God's creative intent, he confirmed that truths themselves admit of differing interpretations, that new research can divulge new facts that need to be incorporated into existing meanings. In fact, all scientific work involves the recurrent disruptions and revisions of previous work. The world is in a constant state of development and so is our knowledge of it.

It is in this context that debates over biblical interpretation and the notion of "evolution in history" can be understood. The biblical scholars of the 1800s were optimistic that their new methods of "higher criticism" could get down to the real meaning of certain texts, without being tainted with theological expectations. Among other things, this led to

---

35 For a short review of this era and its changing view of "teleology," see Crysdale and Ormerod, *Creator God,* 58–64.

36 Charles Darwin, *On the Origin of Species by Means of Natural Selection or the Preservation of Favoured Races in the Struggle for Life* (Mineola, NY: Dover, 2006).

the "quest for the historical Jesus"—the idea that one could get behind all the theological overlay of the Gospel authors in order to discover the "real" Jesus of history.[37] However, as it turned out, not only was it impossible to separate theology and history, the historians themselves seemed to be imposing their own perspectives onto their work. Albert Schweitzer (1875–1965) was insistent in his 1906 book that the search for the historical Jesus was an utter failure. This so-called historical Jesus "is a figure designed by rationalism, endowed with life by liberalism, and clothed by modern theology in an historical garb."[38] In a similar vein, George Tyrell in 1909, in reference to the work of Adolf von Harnack, commented, "The Christ that Harnack sees, looking back through nineteen centuries of Catholic darkness, is only the reflection of a Liberal Protestant face, seen at the bottom of a deep well."[39]

The cultural upshot of all this was the gradual but insistent recognition that meanings themselves change. Method in the hard sciences incorporates an assumption of growing and changing development of ideas. The softer human sciences such as historical scholarship—including biblical scholarship—had to recognize the added complexity of contemporary meaning-makers interpreting human meaning from other times and places. For the church this raised questions about whether dogma  itself can develop. Can the teachings of the church remain true while at the same time adjusting to different eras? Furthermore, growing exploration of non-European locales, combined with energized mission work to these outlying worlds, led to an expanding grasp of the wealth of cultures in the world. Missionaries were forced to adapt the gospel message to foreign ways of life. This, too, posed the question of whether orthodox teachings can bend and adapt to alternative cultures. In sum, is there any standard of normativity—for the church or for Western culture itself—that can withstand the recognition of historical and cultural relativity?

---

37 The classic review and analysis of this quest was written by Albert Schweitzer. An English translation was published in 1911. For a recent edition of this, see Albert Schweitzer, *The Quest of the Historical Jesus*, ed. John Bowden (Minneapolis: Fortress Press, 2001).

38 See http://www.southerncrossreview.org/48/schweitzer-quest.htm. Accessed May 26, 2015.

39 George Tyrrell, *Christianty at the Crossroads* (London: Longmans, Green and Co., 1909), 49.

# Hidden Interests and the Underside of History

We must enlarge on the role of two other major figures in Western culture in order to fill out this picture of shifting worldviews of the nineteenth century. Karl Marx (1818–1883) was a German scholar trained in philosophy who spent most of his life writing on politics and economics. He illustrates the new attention brought to history itself by the developments discussed above. His great interest lay in formulating how it is that history, particularly political and economic history, unfolds. What characterizes the forces that move societies in one direction or the other? Living in the midst of the Industrial Revolution, his answer had to do with modes of production and the relationship between the capitalists who owned various enterprises and the proletariat who made those enterprises work. Jonathan Wolff explains Marx's theory of history as follows:

> Marx sees the historical process as proceeding through a necessary series of modes of production, characterized by class struggle, culminating in communism. Marx's economic analysis of capitalism is based on his version of the labour theory of value, and includes the analysis of capitalist profit as the extraction of surplus value from the exploited proletariat. The analysis of history and economics come together in Marx's prediction of the inevitable economic breakdown of capitalism, to be replaced by communism.[40]

The importance of Marx in our context is simple enough: he brought attention to the actors in history who are most often ignored, forgotten, or exploited. His was an economic analysis, but it posed the general question: Who is it that history forgets? Just how communism in fact emerged in the twentieth century, and whether it can be attributed to the writings of Karl Marx is not the point; that he revealed the vested

---

40 Jonathan Wolff, "Karl Marx," *The Stanford Encyclopedia of Philosophy* (Summer 2011 Edition), Edward N. Zalta (ed.), at http://plato.stanford.edu/archives/sum2011/entries/marx/. Accessed May 26, 2015.

interests of those with the power of capital and unveiled the plight of those exploited by those interests, is.

A second important figure was Sigmund Freud (1856–1939). Freud, who spent most of his life in Vienna, is considered the father of psychoanalysis. He was trained in medicine but saw himself as a research scientist. As modern science was shifting its methods from nonhuman nature to the human sphere, Freud pioneered research into the mind. Stephen Thorton explains the scientific climate in which Freud worked:

> In most respects, the towering scientific figure of nineteenth century science was Charles Darwin, who had published his revolutionary *Origin of Species* when Freud was four years old. The evolutionary doctrine radically altered the prevailing conception of man—whereas before, man had been seen as a being different in nature from the members of the animal kingdom by virtue of his possession of an immortal soul, he was now seen as being part of the natural order, different from nonhuman animals only in degree of structural complexity. This made it possible and plausible, for the first time, to treat man as an object of scientific investigation, and to conceive of the vast and varied range of human behavior, and the motivational causes from which it springs, as being amenable in principle to scientific explanation. Much of the creative work done in a whole variety of diverse scientific fields over the next century was to be inspired by, and derive sustenance from, this new worldview, which Freud with his enormous esteem for science, accepted implicitly.[41]

Freud was particularly interested in what caused abnormal behavior, the field of mental illness. He was sure that causes could be found, and proposed that those causes came from deep inside the mind, due to experiences of early childhood that had been repressed. He explored and refined concepts of the unconscious, made infantile sexuality central to his explanatory framework, and showed that conscious behavior often

---

41 Stephen P. Thorton, "Sigmund Freud," *The Internet Encyclopedia of Philosophy*, at http://www.iep.utm.edu/freud/#H3. Accessed May 26, 2015.

revealed repressed urges of which the subject was not even aware. These unconscious events or feelings could not be brought to consciousness except through protracted psychoanalysis. Dreams and free association of images held clues to connections deep within the psyche and could serve, through careful therapy, to bring old crises to the fore. He saw all human actions, personal dreams, and even cultural artifacts as imbued with symbolic meaning.

While Freud's claim that he had introduced a fully scientific explanation of the mind continues to elicit debate, there is no question that he influenced Western culture tremendously. While Marx exposed the vested interests of capital owners, Freud showed that conscious motives are not always what they seem. With these two thinkers we have introduced into public discourse the notion that "what you see is not always what you get." There may be hidden intentions driving both social systems and interpersonal relations. This idea initiated a cultural element of suspicion when considering all systems of thought or behavior.

Furthermore, these two thinkers illustrate the move toward considering the victims of social or psychic systems. History—whether political and economic narratives or personal life stories—has always been written by those with power and public voice. Marx and Freud drew attention to an "underside" to these histories: Marx by highlighting the exploitation of workers necessary for capital expansion and Freud by underscoring unconscious forces at work in mental abnormalities. At the same time, the mid to late 1800s saw the rise of the women's rights movement—enshrined in Canada and the United States by the women's suffrage campaign—as well as the burgeoning of calls for the abolition of slavery in the U.S. These concerns carried over into waves of feminism and calls for racial civil rights in the twentieth century. On many fronts, then, the idea that there were social groups or individuals who were victims on the underside of dominant social forces came into public view.

A final element in this cultural transition was World War I and its debilitating effect on morale in the Western world. The rise of modern science and the age of reason brought with them great optimism on all fronts. There seemed to be no inquiry into the natural world that would not yield promising results. The new historical consciousness led to critical methods of uncovering meanings from the past. Scholarship in literature and the humanities found new horizons in the nineteenth century. The invention of the steam engine and other innovative technologies created new economic opportunities, both in urban centers and on the frontiers of North America.

All this optimism came to a grinding halt with the advent of war in Europe in 1914. Begun in August of 1914, the war lasted till the armistice of November 11, 1918. The opposing sides were the Allies (Great Britain, France, and Russia) against Germany and the Austro-Hungarian forces, but it eventually drew into its conflict the United States and the Ottoman Empire, with significant contributions of forces from Canada, Australia, and New Zealand. In the end, more than 70 million military personnel participated in one of the largest and deadliest wars in history. Over 9 million combatants were killed, casualties made more gruesome by technological advances and strategic stalemates. Four empires were destroyed—the Ottoman, German, Austro-Hungarian, and Russian. The aftermath of the war led to social trauma across borders, the Russian Revolution, and, eventually, the rise of Nazism. Not only was history a subject for skeptical scholarly reflection, by 1920 it was very clearly not a matter of automatic progress.

# Conclusion

This long whirlwind tour through the history of ideas in the modern era has brought us to the edge of "post"-modernity. The optimism of the age of reason has been dismantled, not only by World War I, but by repeated genocides, insurgencies, and wars, along with economic fraud, political scandal, and domestic violence. The optimism about reason faces disillusionment as well from the discovery of bias and prejudice in human knowing and doing, often at levels below conscious awareness. Globalization and critical history have revealed a plethora of norms and values, such that some kind of analysis and assessment of values is required. No longer can theology speak in one voice, assuming a homogenous audience. In the next chapter we will take up some of the questions that all this raises for Christian theology, on our way to returning to the topic of atonement in our current context.

# 5

## What Does All of This Mean for Theology?

In the last chapter, we traversed five hundred years of changing ideas and their cultural impacts. In this chapter we will address more fully the questions that these shifts in Western culture raise for Christian theology. What is the nature of theology after the "turn to the subject" and on what basis can we make normative claims given historical and cultural diversity? These are big issues beyond the scope of this work, but we will speak to some foundational elements in theology in general before gathering up some specific pieces of atonement theology that are salient to our larger project.

## Challenges for Theology Today

In the introduction to his book *Method in Theology*, Bernard Lonergan (1904–1984) claims, "Theology mediates between a cultural matrix and the significance and role of religion within that matrix."[1] He further notes that we have now moved beyond a *normative* view of culture to an *empirical* one. In the earlier, classicist view, culture was singular and normative—it was what all aspired to become (and was Anglo-European). Now, the notion of culture is empirical, meaning that any culture or subculture simply is what it is. It is a matter for investigation; one needs to determine just what norms and expectations are operative in that particular social group in that specific time and place. Theology is thus no longer singular. If it is to mediate religious meanings to the world, it must do so by taking stock of particular contexts, analyzing past theologies in order to bring forward what is most authentic in them, and learning to communicate these valid meanings in effective ways in the here and now.

Let us highlight several features involved in this process of contemporary theological work. A first element is implicit in this shift away from a normative view of culture. This is the question of norms themselves. Postmodern human science works with the empirical notion of culture, necessarily setting aside the presumption of those outside a culture to question its norms. This functions historically as well. While critical history has unveiled plenty of bias, prejudice, and injustice and is always skeptical about the vested interests of the victors who have written history, what serves as the ground of authenticity by which we can determine valid from invalid social practices? The postmodern practice of deconstructing meanings to find the underlying interests at work leaves open the question of whose perspective is the right one, and how we would account for it.

Second, these questions of bias and objectivity are part of what arises with the turn to the subject outlined in the previous chapter. Kant appealed to structures of the mind whereby we process what we perceive with our senses, but did not believe that we could ever get beyond these mental structures to a "mind-independent" reality. Kant set the stage for the philosophical debates that followed in subsequent centuries: What processes are involved in knowing? Can we know anything at all in an accurate way? Can we know anything about God in a way that would yield valid truth claims? A full account of the many alternative positions is not possible here. But at the very least we need to note that theology

1 Bernard Lonergan, *Method in Theology* (New York: Seabury Press, 1972), xi.

today takes a stand, implicitly or explicitly, not only on propositional claims about God and God's relation to the world, but on the capacity of humans to know anything accurately. Different approaches to theology today have, at base, differing assumptions about knowing, particularly, about religious experience and its role in generating theological claims. Epistemology is basic to theology.[2]

Third, modern scientific methods, including those applied to human studies, brought with them an assumption that everything could be explained according to natural causes. Even religious experience could be reduced to a level of explanation that did not require adverting to the divine. Modern science is *empirical* in that it begins and ends with appeals to evidence, whether natural phenomenon or textual data. It has carried with it an *empiricism*, the philosophical assumption that knowledge comes only from sense experience.[3] This is tied to a metaphysical *naturalism*, a position that maintains that reality is only a matter of natural forces and that nothing exists beyond the natural world.[4] These are pervasive assumptions in the modern world, to the point that in the middle of the twentieth century, theologians were proclaiming, "God is dead."[5] In light of this strong cultural supposition, religious commitment is often considered the domain of those who are clinging to a primitive worldview or of those who are mentally unstable. If theology is indeed to mediate between religion and its cultural matrix in this climate, it will need to give an apologia for taking the supernatural realm seriously.

Fourth, postmodern culture is attentive to suffering in a way that earlier eras were not. This means that the plight of victims has become salient. These persons may have suffered physical, psychological, or sexual violence or bullying, but in any case one can no longer presume that the dominant culture and its personae are the best authorities for interpreting the meaning of a situation. Alternative narratives can and

---

2 Note that some would disagree with this last statement, in effect rejecting the turn to the subject. But that in itself is a response to the epistemological question.

3 See http://en.wikipedia.org/wiki/Empiricism. Accessed May 28, 2015.

4 See John Jacobs, "Naturalism" at http://www.iep.utm.edu/naturali/. Accessed May 28, 2015. This aspect of modern culture is the main focus of Charles Taylor, *Sources of the Self: The Making of the Modern Identity* (Cambridge, MA: Harvard University Press, 1989).

5 See John T. Elson, "Is God Dead?" *Time Magazine*, April 8, 1966. See also Gray, Patrick. "'God Is Dead' Controversy." New Georgia Encyclopedia, http://www.georgiaencyclopedia.org/articles/arts-culture/god-dead-controversy. Accessed August 6 2013.

should be told, not only about the present but about the past. This has an impact on theology because it means that the retrieval of past teachings and practices in the church cannot be taken at face value. Some criterion of authenticity must be delineated in order to discern valid theological meanings from distorted or merely inconsequential claims. It affects theology in the present because the tension between victims and perpetrators is a complex one. Coercive use of power versus the empowerment of human agents for relational flourishing has to be carefully analyzed.

Fifth, the new salience of victims and power relations brings to the fore another element inherent in a theology for our times. It must address the systemic nature of human life and culture. Whereas in some earlier ecclesiastical circles the focus lay on the individual, his relationship with God, or her hope of a future in God's presence, the fact that we are intimately immersed in a community of intersubjectivity can no longer be ignored. Not only are we inherently relational and irretrievably conditioned by our communities, it is now clear that evil has its systemic side. Social sin as well as individual sin needs to be attended to.

Finally, the different realms of meaning—common sense, theory, and interiority (the role of the subject in knowing and doing)—need to be distinguished. These are different ways of understanding our worlds but are not necessarily in conflict. There is the personal appropriation of a biblical passage as well as the careful exegesis that puts it in historical and literary context. Beyond these two foci there is also the question of the exegete herself and the methods by which she can most accurately and authentically do her work. Discussing exegetical method is not doing exegesis, and exegesis is not the same as personal appropriation of a text. All three are valid, but need to be distinguished so that exegesis does not replace personal faith reflection, piety does not shy away from critical questions, and neither overlooks the knowing and reflecting agent involved.

## New Foundations, New Tasks

Prior to *Method in Theology,* in a concise article published in 1968, Lonergan addresses many of these challenges.[6] He reviews much of the history that we traversed in the previous chapter and alludes to historical

---

6 Bernard J. F. Lonergan, "Theology in Its New Context," in *Second Collection*, ed. William F. J. Ryan and Bernard J. Tyrrell (London: Darton, Longman, and Todd, 1974), 55–68.

and cultural relativity as well as the recognition that humans create their own futures. He discusses this as the "constitutive role of meaning in human living":

> It is the fact that acts of meaning inform human living, that such acts proceed from a free and responsible subject incarnate, that meanings differ from nation to nation, from culture to culture, and that, over time, they develop and go astray. Besides the meanings by which man apprehends nature and the meanings by which he transforms it, there are the meanings by which man thinks out the possibilities of his own living and makes his choice among them. In this realm of freedom and creativity, of solidarity and responsibility, of dazzling achievement and pitiable madness, there ever occurs man's making of man.[7]

We can see examples of this constitutive meaning in both individual and corporate lives. Young adults are who they are by virtue of their ethnic, cultural, and personal upbringings. Yet they also contribute to their own futures. A bright young man raised in northern India avails himself of the opportunity to do graduate study in the United States. He forestalls his parents' attempts to introduce him to eligible young women on his return visits to India and decides instead to marry an American and develop a professional life in the American Northwest. North American society itself can undergo a shift in habits when there is a multigenerational recognition of the effects that burning of fossil fuels has on the atmosphere. Local food movements can lead consumers to a greater awareness of farmers in their regions. Personal and communal habits develop and alter options for the future, in both deleterious and beneficial ways.

In light of this way in which human persons and groups constitute the meanings by which they live, Lonergan takes a new approach to divine revelation. Revelation can now be understood as God's entry into this meaning-making. God reveals Godself by entering into the creativity of humankind making itself and its future. It follows that the task of theology goes well beyond merely cataloguing truths about God. "For

---

7 Ibid., 61.

revelation is God's entry into man's making of man, and so theology not only has to reflect on revelation, but also it has somehow to mediate God's meaning into the whole of human affairs."[8]

This new, dynamic approach to theology requires a renewed foundation. The medieval metaphysical synthesis, while innovative and adequate for its time, will no longer do. We could say the same for older versions of biblical theology. But what is the character of this new foundation? It cannot be a set of propositions or principles as these are themselves artifacts of previous ages. Instead, Lonergan looks to the foundation of modern science. This foundation is, likewise, not in the conclusions scientists draw, since these discoveries themselves are being ever improved. Rather, the foundation of modern science lies in its method—the practices of observation, hypothesis, verification, ever refined by increasingly better technologies that aid these operations. At the base of these operations is the functioning scientist herself and her own native urge to understand, to understand correctly, and to further purify and expand what she has come to grasp already.

So the foundation of the modern scientific enterprise lies in the enquiring subject himself, in the questions that drive him toward an ever more accurate grasp of the realities he is seeking to understand. And these queries incorporate within them implicit norms—the norms of intelligibility, truth, and value. The very enterprise of science presumes the value of enquiry, as well as the assumption that the world makes sense and can be grasped correctly. The scientific enterprise is grounded in "incarnate subjects" who operate according to innate norms that both drive their enquiries and indicate when such enquiries have come to a sufficient end.

What, then, of the foundation of theology? Lonergan claims that it lies in the conversion that underpins all religious living. Just as the foundation of modern science lies in the very concrete operations of inquiry in the scientist herself, so the ground of theology lies in the concrete religious experience of the theologian himself. Abstract and universal statements may become the fruits of the theological enterprise, but the foundation lies not in these abstractions but in lived religious transformation.

---

8 Ibid., 62.

For conversion occurs in the lives of individuals. It is not merely a change or even a development; rather, it is a radical transformation on which follows, on all levels of living, an interlocked series of changes and developments. What hitherto was unnoticed becomes vivid and present. What had been of no concern becomes a matter of high import. So great a change in one's apprehensions and one's values accompanies no less a change in oneself, in one's relations to other persons, and in one's relations to God. . . . The convert apprehends differently, values differently, relates differently because he has become different. The new apprehension is not so much a new statement or a new set of statements, but rather new meanings that attach to almost any statement. It is not new values so much as a transvaluation of values. In Pauline language, "When anyone is united to Christ, there is a new world; the old order has gone, and a new order has begun" (2 Cor. 5:17).[9]

Though such conversions are intensely personal, they are not entirely private. They can be shared as part of a community, which aids in working out the implications of such conversions for practical living. What is communal can be handed down through time and become historical. So Lonergan arrives at his conclusion about the enterprise of theology in a new, empirical age:

Now theology, and especially the empirical theology of today, is reflection on religion. It follows that theology will be reflection on conversion. But conversion is fundamental to religion. It follows that reflection on conversion can supply theology with its foundation and,

---

9  Ibid., 65–66. Note that Lonergan is here referring to an empirical fact. Indeed religious experience does occur and this is a matter that needs to be understood not just by theologians. Anyone in the human sciences—sociology, anthropology, psychology, political science—needs to give some intelligible account of it. Likewise, its ubiquity can be the ground for interreligious understanding. Plenty of dialogue needs to take place about the many ways in which such religious experience is expressed and practiced but the basic fact of such religious experience nevertheless sets a basis on which such dialogue might take (and has taken) place.

indeed, with a foundation that is concrete, dynamic, personal, communal, and historical.[10]

Let us explore this idea of conversion in more detail. Lonergan develops this notion of conversion by elaborating on *religious, moral,* and *intellectual* conversions while Robert M. Doran has extended Lonergan's analysis to include *psychic* conversion.[11] We will review religious and moral conversions briefly and then discuss psychic and intellectual conversions at greater length.

*Religious* conversion is the "other worldly falling in love" discussed above. It is a dynamic undertow of consciousness in which our deepest desires find fulfillment in an unrestricted surrender to the ultimately transcendent. As such it is a manifestation of grace: we cannot create in ourselves an apprehension of the ultimate. This felt fulfillment of our deepest desires comes to us, it is given. It can be conscious but not known, not thematized until we reflect on what it is that moves us beyond ourselves in yearning and desire. "Though not a product of our knowing and choosing, it is a conscious dynamic state of love, joy, peace, that manifests itself in acts of kindness, goodness, fidelity, gentleness, and self-control (Gal. 5, 22)."[12]

*Moral* conversion involves coming to a point when one realizes that mere pleasure or pain are not adequate guides for decision-making. It likewise includes the recognition that we are responsible for the persons we become. "So we move to the existential moment when we discover for ourselves that our choosing affects ourselves no less than the chosen or rejected objects, and that it is up to each of us to decide for himself what he is to make of himself . . . then moral conversion consists in opting for the truly good, even for value against satisfaction when value and satisfaction conflict."[13] This recognition is a long way from moral perfection and it implies an extended process of weeding out prejudice and developing habits of care for others. Nevertheless, it sets the groundwork for creation of character by taking responsibility for "man's making of man" in our own lives. It entails choosing ourselves as moral agents

---

10 Ibid., 67.

11 See Lonergan, *Method in Theology,* 240–44, and Robert M. Doran, *Theology and the Dialectics of History* (Toronto: University of Toronto Press, 1990), chap. 2.

12 Lonergan, *Method in Theology,* 106.

13 Ibid., 240.

and becoming accountable for our own moral development in lieu of merely drifting through life.

*Psychic* conversion has to do with the boundary between the conscious and the unconscious. Consciousness involves the entire arena of experience to which we are self-present but to which we have not necessarily attended; unobjectified experience that is *conscious* but not *known*. The *unconscious* involves the assortment of neural transmitters of which we are entirely unaware. It is energy at its physical, chemical, and biological levels. The psyche serves to pattern this unconscious neural manifold into images, symbols, feeling complexes, and the like, which have an "elemental luminosity" that, in turn, is oriented toward the further integration of knowing and acting. In the best possible case, this sensitive experience provides the energy of willingness as well as the images that serve to catalyze insight and action. This optimal situation is hampered, like all our living, on two accounts. The first is our finitude, such that we simply cannot process all the possible material that exists in this energized unconscious, just as we cannot possibly ask all the questions or undertake all the projects we might deem important. So some key catalysts may lie unexplored. Secondly, there is the fact of sin, whereby damage done to us in interpersonal relations, often fostered through generations of power differentials and oppressive cultural or economic systems, penetrates even to the level of what is allowed to emerge and what remains buried.

Because of our finitude, some kind of "censor" is needed to serve as a gatekeeper for what emerges into consciousness and what lies dormant. Otherwise we would go mad. Because of sin, this censor often serves a dysfunctional role, prohibiting us from accessing the very resources we need in order to understand correctly and decide prudently how to act. We get caught in a moral impotence in which the very materials we need to generate willingness or have the insights needed to change our lives are blocked.

Psychic conversion is thus another instance of grace. It involves a transformation of the censor from a repressive to a constructive role. Bob Doran puts it as follows:

> The process of liberation from oppressive patterns of experience is ineffectual unless feelings are touched and stirred by the movement that brings healing insight.

For the psyche is the locus of the embodiment of inquiry, insight, reflection, judgment, deliberation, and decision, just as it is the place of the embodiment of the oppressive forces from which we can be released by such intentional operations. . . . To the extent that our psychic sensitivity is victimized by oppression, the embodiment of the spirit is confined to an animal habitat, fastened on survival, intent on the satisfaction of its own deprivation of the *humanum*. To the extent that the psyche is released from oppressive patterns, the embodiment of the spirit is released into a human world, and indeed ultimately to the universe of being. A true healing of the psyche would dissolve the affective wounds that block sustained self-transcendence; it would give the freedom required to engage in the constitution of the human world.[14]

Like any other conversion, the transformation by which one's censor becomes healing and constructive comes as an effect of grace, often of falling in love, whether with another person or with God. Such falling in love not only transforms one's values and transforms one's knowing, it reorients the spontaneous patterns of one's psyche. It reorders one's emotive habits toward faith, hope, and love, and these become concretely embodied in new patterns of neural energy. Where one lived previously according to reactive impulse, one is now freed to make intentional choices and choose deliberate values.[15]

*Intellectual* conversion has to do with assumptions we make about how we know. It is not about expanding knowledge with new ideas but about appropriating what we already do when we grasp truths. It involves

the elimination of an exceedingly stubborn and misleading myth concerning reality, objectivity, and human knowledge. The myth is that knowing is like looking, that objectivity is seeing what is there to be

---

14 Doran, *Theology,* 61–62.

15 Note how important psychic conversion is then in religious living, since so much religious meaning operates at the symbolic level. It is thus integral to an adequate and authentic theology and practice of atonement in our day.

seen and not seeing what is not there, and that the real is what is out there now to be looked at.[16]

In contrast to this myth, Lonergan asserts:

> Knowing, accordingly, is not just seeing; it is experiencing, understanding, judging, and believing. The criteria of objectivity are not just the criteria of ocular vision; they are the compounded criteria of experiencing, of understanding, of judging, of believing. The reality known is not just looked at; it is given in experience, organized and extrapolated by understanding, posited by judgment and belief.[17]

We can relate this to the questions about knowing addressed in the previous chapter, questions arising with the recognition of the role of the subject in knowing that arose with the Enlightenment. In contemporary Western culture there have been several answers to these questions about how and whether we can know anything accurately. The *naïve realist* insists that, of course, we can know reality; all we have to do is get a good look. *Empiricists* likewise believe that objective knowledge is possible but restrict it to sense experience. Both the naïve realist and the empiricist adopt the myth to which Lonergan objects above. Others, whom we might call *constructivists*, recognize that a lot more goes on in the mind than just "looking"; they acknowledge the further role of understanding in relation to sense experience. But they believe that the mind imposes on sense experience its own constructs, and so the "really real" can never be ascertained with any degree of confidence. Finally, a *critical realist*, like the naïve realist, realizes that we do, often, grasp reality correctly. But this realism is "critical" because it adverts to the processes of seeking understanding—trying to make sense of what is sensed—as well as those of judging—determining which of many

---

16 Lonergan, *Method in Theology*, 238. For the application of this myth to the topic of women and knowing, see Cynthia S. W. Crysdale, "Expanding Lonergan's Legacy: Belief, Discovery and Gender," in *Christian Identity in a Postmodern Age*, ed. Declan Marmion (Dublin: Veritas, 2005), 65–90, and idem, "Women and the Social Construction of Self-Appropriation," in *Lonergan and Feminism*, ed. Cynthia Crysdale (Toronto: Univ. of Toronto Press, 1994), 88–113.

17 Lonergan, *Method in Theology*, 238.

possible explanations is the right one—and believing—trusting others who have wisdom or expertise.

It is this critical realism that is the fruit of the conversion that Lonergan calls intellectual conversion. It is a conversion because it involves a radical change of horizon. And it is a change of horizon that is grounded in "self-appropriation." Intellectual conversion involves affirming that one does know some things accurately. Further, one affirms this by attending to what one does every day as one makes sense of the world around and within him. This attention to what we in fact do all the time is the empirical grounding of this position on knowing. And this position is liberating because it means that truth is the fruit of authentically following through on that to which we are attuned already: asking questions, making sense of experience, checking to make sure that what we discern is indeed correct, and following through on the decisions requisite to that knowing.[18]

An example of how this critical realism impacts theology concerns the first chapter of Genesis. A *naïve realist* takes the story literally, assuming that the narrative is an accurate account of what God did on a series of days in the past. An *empiricist* knows that this is not the case, but since these "days" have been superseded by scientific explanations, the entire enterprise of religious meaning involved here is rejected as outdated nonsense. A *constructivist* acknowledges that the author and the readers are moving well beyond literal claims, but focuses on how authors and readers construct their meanings, assuming that these are merely cultural artifacts without any truth warrants at all. A *critical realist* recognizes the knowing subject—author or reader—as a person driven by the innate need to create meaning and to understand others' meaning accurately. This approach to Genesis 1 seeks to accurately grasp the meanings lying within and behind the text in order to uncover the truths that the text is trying to convey. A simplistic adoption of the literal meaning—whether endorsing it or rejecting it as antiquated—overlooks the subjects involved: both the author trying to accurately convey meaning about God and his relation to creation and the interpreter using

---

18 This describes our knowing when we are figuring things out for ourselves. In fact, in addition to this knowing through discovery, there is much that we know through simply believing others who are reliable. See Lonergan, *Method in Theology*, 41–47, and Cynthia S. W. Crysdale, "Heritage and Discovery: A Framework for Moral Theology," *Theological Studies* 63 (2002): 559–78.

her operations to do more than just notice marks on a page. The need within the interpreter herself to make sense of the text, and to grasp accurately what it is saying about its subject matter, ground a confidence that the truth of what the text is saying can indeed be known.[19]

This example leads us into the question, then, of the specific tasks involved in a theology in which meaning-making in all its cultural and historical manifestations is now acknowledged. Because religious living, grounded in conversion, has yielded multiple meanings through time and in various cultures, theology now has two kinds of jobs to do. A first set of tasks seeks to retrieve authentic meaning from the past. A second set of tasks takes these truths of the past and mediates them to a present context.[20]

The first job—of retrieving the past—Lonergan delineates as involving four distinct tasks. *Research* involves gathering the data—whether manuscripts or other artifacts—and ensuring their authenticity. *Interpretation* entails making sense of these artifacts within their historical and cultural context. What do they mean? What did Paul mean when he spoke of Christ's death as a sacrifice? How did the church in Asia Minor baptize its converts and what did they think it meant? *History* goes beyond mere dates, times, and places (those basics are a matter for research) to the development of meaning. What was going forward from one generation to another? How did the notion of sacrifice evolve in eucharistic practice from the first century to the Middle Ages? How did baptismal practices change in the Eastern Church and what new meanings thus emerged as a result? This historical work will inevitably reveal conflicts—for instance, different meanings ascribed to eucharistic sacrifice or baptismal practice.[21] *Dialectic* engages in sorting out these differences. What is at the heart of these differing theologies? Which are

---

19 Whether or not the interpreter himself is or is not *religiously* converted is not irrelevant here. The more familiar an interpreter is with the topics conveyed in a text—in this case God and God's role as creator and sustainer of the cosmos—the more accurately he can grasp the meanings intended. However, religious conversion in itself will not yield accurate interpretation if the interpreter is overlooking the many steps involved in conveying truth and interpreting it from a text at hand. In other words, while theology is reflection on religious conversion, intellectual conversion has an important if not essential role as well in authentic theology.

20 This is the subject matter of Bernard J. F. Lonergan, *Method in Theology*. For a short explanation of these tasks, which he calls "functional specialties," see chapter 5.

21 While many of the differences unearthed in historical research will seem negligible to us now, at times they were important enough to cause bloodshed.

merely a matter of semantics or cultural evolution and which truly entail irreconcilable oppositions? In our day this task is best illustrated by the work of ecumenical or interfaith dialogue. Some differences are negligible while others indicate true disagreements.[22]

There follows from this work on past traditions the second aspect of theological work: moving theology forward. Once again there are four tasks: *Foundations* involves explicitly addressing the nature of conversion; intellectual, moral, psychic, or religious. It recognizes that doctrines as they have come forward have themselves arisen out of personal, communal, and historical contexts. The shift in horizons that is basic to religious living needs to be delineated clearly so that the criteria by which some developments in history are considered authentic while others are discarded as antiquated or erroneous is objectified.

*Doctrines* express the judgments of fact and judgments of value that have emerged from the work of dialectic, history, interpretation. They clarify what exactly the tradition has brought forward, as grounded in the normative claims that an analysis of religious, moral, intellectual, and psychic conversion has yielded in the work of foundations. Doctrines are affirmations or negations, for example, about God or the work of God in Christ or Christian expectations about life after death. They can also involve other realms of theology such as moral or pastoral theology.[23]

Doctrines raise further questions for understanding. While we may affirm that Christ was indeed entirely human and entirely divine, just how we explain this requires further work. Doctrinal expression may be figurative or symbolic. It may rely on formulas that themselves become the focus of faith (in an idolatrous fashion), or include inconsistencies that need to be ferreted out and resolved. *Systematics* works out appropriate systems of thought, connects one doctrine intelligibly to another, removes inconsistencies, and finds more and better analogies to make sense of the truths of the faith. While doctrines set out to state these truths, systematics seeks to illuminate their intelligibility.

---

22 An example would be recent dialogue between the Lutheran World Federation and the Roman Catholic Church over the doctrine of justification by faith, resulting in a joint declaration issued in Augsburg Germany on October 31, 1999. See The Lutheran World Federation and The Roman Catholic Church, *Joint Declaration on the Doctrine of Justification* (Grand Rapids, MI: Eerdmans, 2000).

23 For example, the statement "It is better to suffer evil than to do evil" is a moral doctrine—a statement of truth about moral living arising from the Christian gospel.

Finally, the work of *communications* is to relate theology to myriad constituencies. There are three tasks here: that of relating theology to other disciplines such as art, literature, or the human or natural sciences; that of transposing theological categories in order to grasp the hearts and minds of persons of all cultures and classes; and adapting theological meanings in order to make full use of diverse media of communication available at particular times and places.[24]

# Retrieving Authentic Atonement Theology

How does any of this play out with regard to the work of this book? We began with problems that the doctrine of the atonement has presented to modern believers averse to any version of salvation that imputes violence onto God. Let us put our objectives in light of the discussion above about theology and its tasks in the modern context. There is no doubt that reconciliation with God is at the heart of the Christian gospel. This doctrine began with a series of kerygmatic claims: that "Jesus died for our sins," that "We are saved by the blood of the cross," and so on. The truth inherent in these phrases as well as the many other images and metaphors at work in the theologizing of the New Testament authors has never been defined in technical language by a church council. Nevertheless, we can insist that the doctrine of atonement is central to the truths handed down from generation to generation of Christian believers.

Recognize, however, that doctrines are answers to questions. If we are to understand doctrines from the past, we need to understand the questions that were being asked at the time. So the task of moving this doctrine forward is not just about gathering up propositions or finding more modern expressions for age-old formulations. It is about understanding the experience—the conversions—of those believers behind the doctrines. What were their experiences, what questions were they asking, and how did they answer them?

For the earliest Christians it seems clear that the devastation of Jesus's execution and the utter surprise of an empty tomb and postresurrection appearances radically altered their horizons. In an effort to tell their stories, they made great attempts to make sense of these events

---

24 See Lonergan, *Method in Theology*, 132.

and their experience. So the "doctrine of the atonement" in its earliest stages was an answer to the question "What was God doing here?" Their answers came in the form of recounting the deeds and sayings of Jesus and preaching the Good News of the kingdom. Eventually this yielded the written word: letters full of images and metaphors (Epistles), treatises on Jewish law and sacrificial practices (Romans and Hebrews), Gospel narratives that used literary devices to instill meaning into chronological events, and an apocalyptic tract (Revelation).

As time went on, the efforts to clarify this key teaching evolved as the gospel took hold in different times and places. The initial "What was God doing here?" became more refined to "How exactly did these events bring about a reconciliation between sinful humankind and God?" In chapter three we gave a very brief review of some of this questioning in the patristic era and its many further images, such as that of God paying a ransom to the devil. With Anselm the question became more theoretical as he sought out "necessary reasons" for both the Incarnation and the Crucifixion. Common sense shifted into theory. The question of the means by which God reconciled humankind to Godself continued apace, presuming Anselm's work on satisfaction but gradually narrowing the question to "What is it about the Crucifixion that brings reconciliation?" To the degree that the answer was "God killed Jesus as a punishment for sin in our place" divine violence began to insert itself into the doctrine. This focus on suffering as itself the agent of salvation carried much of the tradition on atonement doctrine over many centuries, not only at the theoretical level but also in practical piety, art, symbol, and literature.

Our historical review has been meager at best. Nevertheless, we have been engaging in both interpretation and history, relying on many other scholars to aid us in understanding texts and determining what was going forward as meanings evolved over time.[25] We have not undertaken dialectic in the detailed way that one would if one were to compare and contrast different authors or practices or sets of meanings as this doctrine moved through Christian history. Rather, we have taken our starting point from a conflict that has become clear in recent decades, an apparent conflict between two very core doctrines of Christian faith: the doctrine of atonement and the doctrine of God. This latter doctrine has

---

25 We have very much taken research for granted, presuming upon the work of manuscript evaluators, archeologists, linguists, cultural historians, and biblical exegetes.

at its center the idea that God is all loving and that love is at the heart of the Trinity. So perhaps our question today is "How can we understand the doctrine of the atonement in a way that does not contradict our view of God as all loving and in no way violent?"

While we have used the word "doctrine" repeatedly, our task throughout has not been to determine what is or is not doctrine, but to make sense of it. We are taking the centrality of the doctrine for granted, and asking what intelligibility we can find in it.[26] In that sense we are engaged in the task of systematics: Assuming that "Jesus died for our sins" is indeed at the heart of the gospel, how can we possibly explain this in ways that do not make of God a cruel tyrant or, worse, pit two persons of the Trinity against each other?

Our answer comes from two directions—on the one hand laying the foundation in an understanding of the human subject as oriented toward God and on the other hand gathering up what we have learned from our review of the past theological tradition. The foundational element we have covered in some detail above in discussing religious conversion as an "otherworldly falling in love" in light of moral, intellectual, and psychic conversions.[27] This foundation lies in the grace of God coming to us—first of all in creation itself but further in meeting our deepest yearnings for something beyond us, and in healing the sins that keep us from recognizing God. This grace came in embodied form in the advent of Jesus into history. It is, from beginning to end, about *relationship*— the yearning for it, the healing of it, the ongoing renewal that enlivens it.

What, then, can we glean from our review of the biblical and historical interpretations of this experience of graced love as known in the events of Jesus's life, death, and resurrection? From what good historical research allows us to infer about Jesus's own understanding, we discover

---

26 See Lonergan's published lecture, "The Redemption," in Bernard J. F. Lonergan, *Philosophical and Theological Papers, 1958–1964*, ed. Crowe Frederick E., Robert M. Doran, and Robert C. Croken, *Collected Works of Bernard Lonergan*, vol. 6 (Toronto: University of Toronto Press, 1996), section 3.

27 Religious conversion without intellectual conversion can lead to a fundamentalism that is not in touch with the role of the person as contributing to interpretation of biblical sources or to the process of theologizing itself. Religious conversion without moral conversion can lead to tyranny or coercion within religious circles, and/or a failure to take stock of the human agent as contributing to the meanings and values of human living. Religious conversion without psychic conversion can produce unreflective prejudice and bigotry as well as psychological oppression.

that Jesus believed his mission was to initiate a new work of God in the world—the eschatological kingdom of God. He anticipated his own death at the hands of those enthralled with power, but believed that his tribulation on behalf of the faithful would mark the beginning of the restoration of Israel to its proper role as a light to all nations.

From Paul we can take several significant points. First and foremost, the power of Paul's own conversion and that of his followers stands behind everything he says, as he tries to make sense of his "resurrection" in light of Christ's own. Throughout his pastoral theology lies the conviction that it is God who initiates the reconciliation with humankind. It is in light of this appeal to God's grace that God's judgment of sin and God's purpose in Jesus's mission and death must be interpreted. In other words, the key to understanding atonement for Paul is that it begins and ends with *relationship* and *grace*. When the covenant relationship with Israel broke down, God repaired and restored it over and over again. When the Torah ultimately failed to bring about the desired relationship, God moved history into a new era, a new covenant, founded in his son, Jesus the Christ. While humans once again rejected this messenger, even to the point of executing him, God nevertheless initiated something new—a new covenant founded on the sacrifice represented by Christ's death on the cross and evidenced in the victory of the resurrection.

Furthermore, atonement is not about something that happened in the past. Rather, we *participate* in Jesus's death and resurrection now. As Jesus was made new by being raised from the dead, so we are made new each day by dying to sin and its power over us. Our repeated resurrections restore our relationship with God and others over and over again. Atonement is not a matter of some status we have attained before God but is about new life in relationship through the acceptance of God's gift. We do look forward to a fulfillment of this new life in a future encounter with the risen Lord. But that will be a consummation of what already is ours—freedom from the life of sin.

Paul's emphasis on *relationship, grace,* and *participation* is reflected in the evidence we have of the earliest church's practices of baptism and Eucharist. It seems clear that the disciples remembered the Last Supper and its symbolic meanings in light of Jesus's death. This is reflected in the New Testament account of this event, in both Paul and the synoptic Gospels. While John gives a different account of what occurred on the night before Jesus's died (the washing of the disciples' feet), his entire story is set within a context of eucharistic symbolism and the need for rebirth. Likewise, baptism came to have new significance—beyond that practiced by John the Baptist—in light of Jesus's death and resurrection. It is manifest that the earliest traditions of theologizing about the crucifixion incorporated both baptism and Eucharist as ways that believers could share in the same death and new life that Jesus had experienced. It is, furthermore, evident that Christians who came to believe, from various quarters, over time made these rituals of participation central to community life and worship.

What do we learn from the first centuries of patristic thinking about God's work in Christ? Ireneaus illustrates the struggle of the nascent religion to withstand the mind/body dualism of Greek thought in general and Gnosticism in particular. Ireneaus, like many of his contemporaries, treated the problem of sin by laying emphasis on the Incarnation. Christ "recapitulated" the creation of Adam yet without sin, opening the door for a new humanity to be in right relation with God. In doing this, Iraneaus established two fundamental principles on which we can rely today. By focusing on the Incarnation in a world that eschewed the "flesh," he asserted that creation itself, our embodiment, and Christ's taking up of embodiment, is all good. Material existence is not a problem that needs to be solved—indeed God himself used it to bring about new life. A corollary, secondly, is that Ireneaus makes it clear that the root of evil lies in disobedience—breaking relationship with God. Hence, spiritual freedom is not about ridding ourselves of evil fleshly existence in favor of some more esoteric spiritual life. Christ reversed Adam's sin in his obedience, because of his great love, handing himself over willingly to the cross, and in so doing defeating the devil.

The theme of *Christus Victor*—that Christ defeated the devil and his hold over humankind—was woven through many theologies of the patristic period, combined with the idea that a ransom was paid in order to free us from sin. Debates ensued about who received this ransom—God or the devil? The notion of paying a ransom to God was dismissed by Origen since it was the devil who enslaved us to sin. The idea that the devil somehow deserved a ransom became problematic, nevertheless, since it seemed to put God and the devil on an equal footing. Augustine nuanced this tradition in ways that have important ramifications. While the devil's claim to humankind had a certain justice to it, in that Adam did indeed succumb to the temptations of the devil, the devil's appeal to a just ransom in exchange for human release lies far off the mark.

While Ireneaus stressed sin as disobedience rather than embodiment, Augustine goes further to insist that it is a lust for power—the kind of power only God has—that lies at the heart of human transgression. It is precisely this kind of power that the devil yearns for but does not have. What lies at the center of the Christian gospel is that God defeats the devil's enslavement of humankind not through a direct power struggle but through justice itself. As Augustine put it: "The essential flaw of the devil's perversion made him a lover of power and a deserter and assailant of justice, which means that men imitate him all the more thoroughly the more they neglect or even detest justice and studiously devote themselves to power."[28] By allowing the devil—apparently—to "win" through killing Jesus on the cross, God turns the whole power game upside down. Christ willingly offers himself though he is sinless. When the devil discovers that there is in fact nothing in Jesus deserving of death, yet kills him anyway, his own lust for power is exposed. Augustine's insight is that freedom from the enslavement to sin—being held in the devil's power—arises not as a matter of power but as a reversal of roles due to Chist's willing and justice-loving surrender. Christ's love for humankind, extended to the point of death, exposed the lie of power mongering and revealed instead the true justice of God's love and forgiveness.

With Anselm we have the initial move into theory, an attempt to put logic and systematic reason into the work of God in reconciling humankind to himself. While he left many loose ends, we can at least retain some key elements. First, Anselm takes the dilemma of sin with exceeding seriousness. He does not minimize the destruction caused by the human failure to acknowledge God and give God his due, namely thanks and praise. The fruits of sin are no less than the disruption of the cosmic order—God's providential will for creation, i.e., God's honor. He further understands God's justice in the face of this dilemma to require retribution; the problem of evil needs to be resolved, either through punishment (death) or through some other kind of recompense (satisfaction).

---

28 Augustine, *The Trinity,* ed. John E. Rotelle, trans. Edmund Hill, *The Works of Saint Augustine: A Translation for the 21st Century,* part I, vol. 5 (New York: New York City Press, 1991), 356.

In our contemporary world, the gravity of evil, particularly human cruelty toward others, including creation itself, cannot be overlooked with a liberal optimism. While revenge rarely yields true justice and reconciliation, dismissing justice concerns as trivial or simplistic only perpetuates the problem.

At the same time, it is essential to recognize that the core of Anselm's solution does not lie in further cruelty. While Christ did indeed stand in for us in making the offering we owed to God for our sin, the heart of the matter lies not in punishment but in satisfaction. The core of the matter is not Christ's *death* per se but in Christ's loving willingness to die. Essential to this is the full incarnational reality of Christ. Since Christ was fully human but did not sin, he himself was not subject to death as a punishment for sin. He persevered in living a holy life in spite of the fact that it would lead to his unjust execution. *This* offering, of a holy, loving, and obedient human life regardless of its trajectory toward death, is what saves. The love at the center of this self-offering, not the death or the violence by which it occurred, is the key to redeeming humankind. In our world of deliberate brutality such self-surrender in love serves as a counterpoint to the many solutions to evil that involve disseminating further violence.

# Conclusion

What, then, do we make of the powerful trajectory in popular religion through the ages that focuses directly on Jesus's suffering as the means to salvation? For starters we do not dismiss it as primitive nonsense, since identification with the suffering Christ is such a key component to the participation upon which Paul so strongly insisted. Rather, we adopt a nuanced discernment of what constitutes a healing identification with Christ's suffering that leads to renewed life, over against an oppressive further enslavement. This is where the distinctions that have emerged in the tradition along with our modern analyses of power hegemony and systemic injustice come to bear on determining healthy piety.

We can retrieve the patristic focus on Incarnation to balance out the lopsided attention to the cross as the locus of atonement. Jesus's life, death, and resurrection constitute the atoning work of God, not just his suffering on the cross. Our current cultural focus on universal human rights, the dignity of each person, and the importance of empowering those on the underside of tyrannical systems of meaning and power endorse this retrieval. With Ireneaus we can affirm the goodness of bodily life and curtail any attempt to exacerbate bodily harm as in some way exemplary or salvific. This goes a long way toward challenging any justification of bodily denigration or violence as a means of creating or sustaining social harmony.

Anselm helps us draw the line, however subtle, between punishment and satisfaction; loving self-surrender rather than punishment per se is what serves as an example to be followed by the disciples of Christ. Punishment as revenge rarely produces healing resolutions. While there is nothing good in itself about suffering evil, nevertheless some situations can only be turned around when some group is willing to suffer evil rather than do evil. With Augustine we can note that the victory of the risen Christ—not only in the past but now—comes from loving justice, accepting the consequences of doing so, and thus unmasking the lies and power plays by which so much of the world works. Suffering may come as the result of just loving but suffering does not in itself produce justice, healing, or salvation.

Finally, whatever salvation emerges is the effect of God's work in us, both for our own transformation and as agents of change for others. We cannot manipulate God into loving us through our own efforts, nor can we prescribe and effect systemic change without God's wisdom and guidance. Our job is to participate in the death and resurrection process already at work in our lives and communities, not to seek out further anguish as if that would bring us closer to God.

The key to healthy piety is identification and participation in something God has already done, and is doing, in us. Beginning with our own lives and the struggles in the world around us we find the consequences of basic sin, the pain and suffering that failure to acknowledge and adequately love God has produced. In that place, in that realm, we discover the crucified and risen Lord. Identifying with him is a way of participating with him, through death to new life.

# 6

Transformed Lives
Reconsidered

It is now time to gather together what might be said about the work of God in Jesus's life, death, and resurrection. We have traversed many centuries, gathering up gems from biblical and theological traditions. Our task has not been to determine doctrine but to understand accurately the core of the gospel in relation to our redemption. In this chapter we will give a contemporary account of God's work in Christ "for us and for our salvation." We will conclude with a few examples of lives changed by the grace of God at work through transformed meanings.

## The Incarnate Word:
## God's Offer of Friendship

The Christian gospel proclaims that God was in Christ reconciling the world to Godself. Further, it claims that God was in Christ in a unique way; that the second person of the Trinity was made human in Jesus of Nazareth while remaining at the same time fully God. This is one of the "mysteries" of the faith, not in the sense of a problem to be solved but in the sense of a supernatural reality that we, as finite creatures, will never fully grasp. While there is still much that can be said about such mysteries, Jesus as the incarnate word of God is not our precise focus here. Rather, we ask what his being God and human—two natures in one person in the technical language—yields in terms of reconciliation between humankind and God.

An initial point is that whatever occurred in the Christ event—the birth, life, death, and resurrection of Jesus of Nazareth—it had to do with meaning-making.[1] This is to say that it was not about some "objective" transaction that happened between God and humankind in an abstract way, devoid of human understanding. Nor was it a transaction that happened between two persons of the Trinity. The Christ event was revelatory; it revealed to humankind something about God himself in a way that only a God-man could do. This was revelation as God's entrance into "man's making of man." This communication was not a set of abstract propositions but a concrete human person, Jesus, who so embodied God as to reveal God in a new way. He communicated this meaning through the whole of his personal presence, as experienced by those who met him, who were healed by him, who chose to follow him. He expressed this meaning in words, through preaching and exhortation. And he personified divine meaning in symbolic gestures, such as his entrance ride into Jerusalem, the "cleansing" of the temple, and his actions and words at the Last Supper. Finally, there was the unexpected trajectory of events in the execution, and then resurrection, of this historical person from Nazareth. In all these ways God offered in history a new set of meanings for the struggles of creatures in relation to the Creator.

This meaning-filled offer was given regardless of whether it was accepted or understood. And those who received it had to make sense of their experience. And we, in turn, are dependent on their religious conversions, their "sense-making" of what happened before and after Jesus's death. The point is that, while there are objective facts, and even an

---

1 See Bernard J. F. Lonergan, "The Redemption," in Lonergan *Philosophical and Theological Papers, 1958–1964,* ed. Frederick E. Crowe, Robert M. Doran, and Robert C. Croken, *Collected Works of Bernard Lonergan,* vol. 6 (Toronto: University of Toronto Press, 1996), section 2.

already intended set of meanings to which we can refer, unless the ear-liest followers—and we—discern what was meant and enter into these meanings, reconciliation does not occur. There is no "already-out-there-now-real" atonement that occurs without our engagement. Those who lived at the time, the generations since, and we, must interpret, under-stand, accept or reject certain meanings as correct and constitutive of our lives.

Likewise, if indeed God was working redemption for us in these events, it is not the case that atonement is something that happened way back in time. Rather, there were events, and there were a host of people who found that God was at work in a unique way in these events. These events, this communication of God, changed lives at the time. But it con-tinued to change lives long after the risen Christ left earthly existence. So the church attests not only to the visible mission of the Son in Jesus of Nazareth, but to the invisible mission of the Holy Spirit. The Gospel of John has Jesus promising that he will send another, a comforter and advocate. The author of Luke/Acts portrays the pouring out of the Spirit on the church. Paul adverts regularly to the Spirit's work in believer's lives. So God's offer of new life in relation to him continued, and con-tinues in the community of believers, led by God's Spirit. Atonement is not only a past accomplishment but also a current process.

What is it that God was/is communicating in the Christ event and the ongoing work of the Spirit today? In the classical sense of the word, the incarnation of the second person of the Trinity was an offer of *friend-ship*. Friendship in the modern Ango-European world today is a shallow version of a much deeper meaning in the classical tradition. Friendships today are private, voluntary, informal connections between autonomous individuals. They often form around a task that needs to be done, or fun activities that are shared. These alliances usually come to an end when the relevant tasks or activities end. In addition to these kinds of friend-ships, Aristotle maintained that perfect friendship is based on shared goodness and has permanence. In such relationships, "each alike wish good for the other *qua* good, and they are good in themselves." Further, "And it is those who desire the good of their friends for the friends' sake that are most truly friends, because each loves the other for what he is, and not for any incidental quality."[2] More extensively he says:

---

2 Aristotle, *The Nichomachean Ethics* (London: Penguin, 1976), 205.

> Friendship of this kind is permanent, reasonably enough; because in it are united all the attributes that friends ought to possess. For all friendship has as its object something good or pleasant—either absolutely or relatively to the person who feels the affection—and is based on some similarity between the parties. But in this friendship all the qualities that we have mentioned belong to the friends themselves; because in it there is similarity, etc.; and what is absolutely good is also absolutely pleasant; and these are the most lovable qualities. Therefore it is between good men that both love and friendship are chiefly found and in the highest form.[3]

Thus, to know a friend is to know oneself, and the good person relates to her friend in the same way she relates to herself.

Aquinas extends this deep understanding of friendship to the love that exists between men and women and God:

> Charity signifies not only the love of God, but also a certain friendship with Him; which means, besides love, a certain mutual communion. . . . Now this fellowship of women and men with God, which consists in a certain familiar conversation with Him, is begun here, in this life, by grace, but will be perfected in the future life, by glory; each of which things we hold by faith and hope. So just as friendship with a person would be impossible, if one disbelieved in, or despaired of, the possibility of their fellowship of familiar conversation; so too, friendship with God, which is charity, is impossible without faith, so as to believe in this fellowship and conversation with God, and to hope to attain to the fellowship. Therefore charity is impossible without faith and hope.[4]

---

3  Ibid., 205–6; see M. E. Doyle and Smith, M. K. Smith (2002), "Friendship: Theory and Experience," *The Encyclopaedia Of Informal Education*. http://infed.org/mobi/friendship-some-philosophical-and-sociological-themes/. Accessed June 9, 2015.

4  From Thomas Aquinas, *Summa Theologiae*, Prima Secundae, Question 65, Article 5, as emended by Dr. Jennifer Anne Jackson. Thanks to Dr. Jackson for this reference.

So human friendship involves mutual, benevolent love, committed to some common good. Friendship with God—which is love—is possible but aided in this life by faith and hope. When it comes to God in Godself, properly speaking there are just three friends of God. "God *are* those friends: the Father, the Son, and the Spirit."[5] It is this divine friendship that God became human in order to communicate to mankind; to extend to finite friends the community of intimacy that constitutes God in Godself. Though God did not need to do this, God chose to offer this friendship through a finite, secondary cause, becoming a part of creation itself. Charles Hefling pursues this line of thought:

> In order to mediate divine friendship, such a secondary cause would have to be a friend of God in his or her own right; otherwise this friendship would have to be mediated *to* him or her, and so on *ad infinitum*. The alternative, that is, to an infinite regress, which explains nothing, is an *intermediate friend*. But the right to be God's friend belongs to no created being, no finite person, because commitment to infinite good is by definition supernatural. Humans have no claim to it, no exigence for it. It is natural only to divine persons.[6]

So Jesus of Nazareth the Son of God—in his embodied presence but also in his words, actions, and symbolic gestures—reveals God in a way that invites us into the heart of God's own divine intimacy. This incarnation of God's very own self in history concretizes the graceful offer of God's love that began with creation. Rowan Williams puts this as follows:

> Grace, for the Christian believer, is a transformation that depends in large part on knowing yourself to be seen in a certain way: as significant, as wanted.
>
> The whole story of creation, incarnation, and our incorporation into the fellowship of Christ's body tells us that God desires us, *as if we were God*, as if we were

---

5 Charles Hefling, "Lonergan's *Cur Deus Homo*: Revisiting the 'Law of the Cross,'" in *Meaning and History in Systematic Theology: Essays in Honor of Robert Doran, SJ*, ed. J. D. Dadosky (Milwaukee: Marquette University Press, 2009), 157.

6 Ibid.

that unconditional response to God's giving that God's self makes in the life of the Trinity. We are created so that we may be caught up in this, so that we may grow into the wholehearted love of God by learning that God loves us as God loves God.[7]

God began this in God's gratuitous creation of our universe, expanded the offer of friendship by the visible mission of the Son, and continues diffusing the grace of transforming intimacy through the invisible mission of the Spirit in the community of the faithful.

A further point arises. Was the sending of the Son necessitated by the sinfulness of humankind? Was the grace of friendship that was offered in creation a failure that required a subsequent gesture? In other words, is the Incarnation primarily about redemption? While the Incarnation *is* about redemption, it is not *only* about redemption. God in God's providence understood and understands the full unfolding of history. There are no divine afterthoughts. God's primary purpose in sending the Son was the mediation of friendship, the invitation for humankind to enter the meaning of God's intimacy in a more complete way. As it happens, however, the friends whom God would befriend are *sinners*. "Man's making of man," in which God takes part by becoming human, is no neutral country, as it were. It is enemy territory. There is unfriendliness, decline, the objective social surd."[8]

The principle at work here is that friends love their friends' friends. They love their friends' friends even if those friends are their own enemies. So Tom loves Susan, who is friends with Jack. Tom and Jack have a history of enmity but because of his love for Susan, Tom loves Jack and visa versa. With Jesus the Son of God we have the special case in which the intermediate friend desires for his friends—who in fact are enemies of God—their full flourishing. "Every genuine friend wants for his or her friends what is best for them, as Aristotle pointed out. The intermediate friend of God [the Incarnate Son] will want for *his* friends, who happened to be God's enemies, what is best for them, namely that they should repent and be converted."[9]

7 Rowan Williams, "The Body's Grace," in *Our Selves, Our Souls and Bodies*, ed. Charles Hefling (Boston: Cowley Publications, 1996), 59. Italics in the original.
8 Hefling, "Lonergan's *Cur Deus Homo*," 160.
9 Ibid.

So the Incarnation is not in the first instance about dealing with human sin. It is about the full flourishing of humankind through graced relationship with the divine. But since all of humankind participates in the distortions that are both the causes and the symptoms of sin—deceit, betrayal, greed, self-indulgence, power mongering, and the like—the sending of the Son as an intermediary friend to convey divine friendship is bound to meet its own rejection, a rejection that is the fruit of human self-conceit and lust for power. So understanding the Incarnation as an expression of divine love must be accompanied by a quest for the intelligibility of its outcome in history, namely that Jesus ended up executed as a common criminal, only to be proclaimed a short while later as the Risen Lord.

## Jesus's Death and Resurrection: Transforming Power and Oppression

So what do we make of the fact that this supreme divine communication incorporates what to us seems to be a complete failure, a tragedy of the utmost sort? Let us begin with Lonergan's presentation of the "law of the cross":

> This is why the Son of God became man, suffered and died, and was raised again: Because divine wisdom has ordained and divine goodness has willed, not to do away with the evils of the human race by force, but to convert those evils into a supreme good in keeping with the just and mysterious Law of the Cross.[10]

In this case the "supreme good" that is the ultimate end of this drama is the full friendship with the divine of which we spoke above. But this supremely good intimacy meets its obstacle in the human refusal to be just what being human is—finite creatures with unrestricted longings for that which is *super*natural: a knowledge or good or beauty that transcends human capabilities. The mistaking of this human aspiration for

---

10 Bernard J. F. Lonergan, *The Redemption*, trans. Michael Shields, ed. Robert M Doran, Daniel Monsour, and Jeremy Wilkins, *Collected Works of Bernard Lonergan*, vol. 9 (Toronto: University of Toronto Press, forthcoming), thesis 17.

the transcendent as a goal to be reached by human achievement constitutes the sin of hubris. The capitulation to the limitations of creaturely
existence, the failure to follow the yearning for something beyond, is
the sin of self-abnegation.[11] Either way we fail the test of being human,
and, across generations, hubris and oppression, timidity and self-loathing
become instantiated in communal patterns of meaning and practice.

These distorted patterns leave the entire race in a position of moral
impotence. In order to reorder our lives, we need insights, judgments of
fact, and judgments of value that can lead to the needed changes. But it is
precisely our desire to pursue and enact these that is lacking. At a deeper
level the longing for what is "beyond"—for truth, beauty, loving friendship—is itself truncated, by individual choice and by social ridicule. The
cycle of decline reaches an impasse, whereby "there is no use appealing
to the sense of responsibility of irresponsible people, to the reasonableness of people that are unreasonable, to the intelligence of people that
have chosen to be obtuse, to the attention of people who attend only to
their own grievances."[12]

So the supreme good of intimacy with God needs to be restored.
But this situation of distortion cannot be resolved by human effort alone.
And even a supernatural solution will not be a matter of some direct causality, whereby A simply "fixes" B, since the "surd" of sin is embedded
beyond the point of a simple corrective. Rather than logic, what is needed
is a complete reversal, whereby unwillingness becomes a willing of the
good, selfish obsessions are turned outward to empathy, and obtuseness
is replaced by a pursuit of the truth. This is the stuff of conversion, the

---

11 Over many centuries sin was understood primarily as the first half of this dyad, that is,
sin as pride and hubris. Valeria Saiving Goldstein first pointed out that this is generally
the sin of those who are dominant in a culture, that is, primarily, men. She presented the
notion that, for women, pride is not the primary sin; rather self-deprecation is. Judith
Plaskow picked up this theme and used it to analyze the theology of Reinhold Niebuhr
and Paul Tillich, which she concluded both suffer from this one-sided understanding
of sin as pride. This critique is now commonplace in contemporary discussions of sin.
See Valerie Saiving Goldstein, "The Human Situation: A Feminine View," *Journal of
Religion* 40 (1960): 100–112, and Judith Plaskow, *Sex, Sin, and Grace* (Lanham, MD:
University Press of America, 1980). An overview of this position can be found in Sally
Alsford, "Sin and Atonement in Feminist Perspective," in *Atonement Today*, ed. John
Goldingay (London: SPCK, 1995). My own work reflects this two-sided understanding
of sin and its reversal. See Cynthia S. W. Crysdale, *Embracing Travail: Retrieving the
Cross Today* (New York: Continuum, 1999).

12 Bernard J. F. Lonergan, "Dialectic of Authority," in *A Third Collection*, ed. Frederick E.
Crowe (New York: Paulist Press, 1985), 9.

advent of entirely new horizons whereby the gift of love sheds new light and engenders desire in otherwise deadened hearts.

And such conversions do not come about by force. Force, violence, and revenge only perpetrate what they are trying to eradicate. So we have what Walter Wink has designated the "myth of redemptive violence" with its obverse, the myth of redemptive suffering.[13] Neither violence nor suffering, in themselves, produce the transformation needed to turn social and individual sin around. Instead "divine wisdom has ordained and divine goodness has willed, not to do away with the evils of the human race by force, but to convert those evils into a supreme good in keeping with the just and mysterious law of the cross."[14]

What is the nature of this transformation? As stated above, it is not a solution that comes by logic or direct causality. Because evil is itself radically unintelligible—by definition it does not make sense but is the *absence* of reasonable action—basic sin and its complex consequences must be reversed not "conquered."[15] And paradoxically, this reversal occurs precisely by the exposure of evil for what it is—self-serving lust for power and control. The coming of the One who is divine but human—like us in all things but sin—who *nevertheless* is persecuted, tortured, and executed, makes explicit what is otherwise hidden: the oppressive power behind the lust for control, and the innocence of the victims who suffer at its hands.

Several contemporary approaches to this can fill out the nature of this radical shift. Sebastian Moore in *The Crucified Is No Stranger* provides a modern interpretation of salvation in terms of personal drama. His central insight is that Jesus represents to us the very self that we

---

13 See Walter Wink, *Engaging the Powers: Discernment and Resistance in a World of Domination* (Minneapolis: Fortress Press, 1992), esp. chap. 1. Wink's work is discussed and revised in Crysdale, *Embracing Travail*, 43–46, 53–55. On the myth of redemptive suffering, see Crysdale, *Embracing Travail*, 46, 57, 59.

14 Lonergan, *Redemption*, thesis 17.

15 The Christian tradition, from Augustine forward, has seen evil as the absence of the good. Thus, an act of evil—which Lonergan calls *basic sin*—suffers from a lack of intelligibility. The consequences of this failure of reasonableness can indeed be understood as part of an intelligible causal chain. But the initial failure of will itself cannot be understood because there is no reason behind it. See Bernard J. F. Lonergan, *Insight: A Study of Human Understanding*, ed. Frederick E. Crowe and Robert M. Doran, Collected Works of Bernard Lonergan, vol. 3 (Toronto: University of Toronto Press, 1992), 689–90, and Peter Laughlin, *Jesus and the Cross: Necessity, Meaning, and Atonement* (Eugene, OR: Pickwick Publishers, 2014), 79–87.

are called to be; but it is precisely this self that we refuse to be. "What if Jesus were the representative, the symbol, the embodiment, of this dreaded yet desired self of each of us, this destiny of being human . . . ? The crucifixion of Jesus then becomes the central drama of man's refusal of his true self."[16]

This drama has both its historical component in Jesus's life, death, and resurrection as well as its counterpart in the life of the person being transformed. The key to the historical story is that the cross makes explicit what is otherwise latent. Because of Jesus's purity, because there is no evil in him, all the evil is revealed on the side of those who wish him dead. "The evil thus restricted to the crucifiers becomes an *act*, arising in the human heart and proceeding to its destructive conclusion; an *act*, don't you see, and no longer an *atmosphere*."[17]

It is this act of destruction of the pure One that makes explicit not only Jesus's innocence but the perpetrators' maliciousness. Not only power mongering but the rationalization of it and the resentment toward those who are not caught in its vise is made plain:

> Evil is the inability of the death-wish to simply be a death-wish: its necessity to justify itself by removing the very *grounds* for requiring of us a more intensely personal life. This shows itself in the resentment that is sometimes felt in the presence of an exceptionally good and courageous man. The desire to remove him is the desire to remove an unusually eloquent piece of evidence for the fact that we are called to full personhood. The most passionately protected thing in us is our mediocrity, our fundamental indecision in respect of life. Its protection will require, and will not stop at, murder.[18]

The point is that the solution to the problem of evil is to let evil expand to its full extent—the undeserved execution of the one purely innocent victim. In allowing evil to be taken to its full extreme, it is exposed as ultimately powerless. The resurrection makes a lie of the

---

16 Sebastian Moore, *The Crucified Is No Stranger* (London: Darton, Longman and Todd, 1977), x. Moore's work is discussed in Crysdale, *Embracing Travail*, 8–11, 26–34.

17 Moore, *Crucified*, 2.

18 Ibid., 13.

supposed control that the powers of the day believed they had. In the end, evil is unmasked for what it is and the greater power of love is manifested in the creation of life out of death.

This is the "objective" meaning of the Jesus event: that God came to offer divine friendship through an intermediary friend who was himself a divine friend of God. This was an offer to humankind even in the midst of its alienation from its God-given personhood and from God. The embodied divine offer was himself rejected and the one and only fully innocent human being was resented, feared, mocked, and killed. Rather than spelling the failure of this divine offer, this travesty merely exposed human hubris for what it is. The fact that such evil is not the last word, that even the worst possible evil—the murder of God himself—can be transformed into new life constitutes the offer of new life to all, those who suffer evil and those who do it. We avail ourselves of this offer when we discover ourselves in this story, as both perpetrators of "murder" and as victims of it.

Walter Wink takes a similar approach, focusing more on destructive social systems, which he designates simply as the "Powers." Jesus's life was one of challenge to those with social and cultural privilege, what he calls the "Domination System." He cites Abraham Heschel's remark that the Hebrew prophets were the first people in history to regard a nation's reliance on force as evil.[19] Jesus follows in this line of prophetic proclamation and living. Through his preaching, his concern for the marginalized, his treatment of women, his breaking of ritual practices, and his command to love one's enemies, Jesus embodied an alternative to domination. The most radical element of his resistance is that he defined his life's meaning according to his identity as a beloved Son empowered by divine relationship.

Jesus's death, then, becomes the logical conclusion of the radical way he lived. It also serves as the ultimate unveiling (apocalyptic) event. In one sense his mission failed. But by refusing to succumb, even in the face of death, to the Power's definition of him, Jesus exposed the Powers for what they were. Wink puts it thus:

---

19 Wink, *Engaging the Powers,* 45. He is citing Abraham Heschel, *The Prophets* (New York: Harper and Row, 1969), 1:166.

Here was a person able to live out to the fullest what he felt was God's will. He chose to die rather than compromise with violence. The Powers threw at him every weapon in their arsenal. But they could not deflect him from the trail that he and God were blazing. Because he lived thus, we too can find our path.

Because they could not kill what was alive in him, the cross also revealed the impotence of death. Death is the Power's final sanction. Jesus at his crucifixion neither fights the darkness nor flees under cover if it, but goes with it, goes into it. He enters the darkness freely, voluntarily. The darkness is not dispelled or illuminated. It remains vast, untamed, void. But he somehow encompasses it. It becomes the darkness of God. It is now possible to enter any darkness and trust God to wrest from it meaning, coherence, resurrection.[20]

This latter point is a key one. God neither wills Jesus's death nor does he "solve" the problem of sin and its consequences. God *allows* Jesus's crucifixion knowing that it will constitute a part of the whole of the transformation of evil into good.[21] And God *encompasses* the death and darkness that result from human alienation and its results. God is able to wrest from these a transformed horizon of new life for his human creatures, indeed for the entire creation. But God solves the problem of evil, not by force or violence or revenge, but by embracing the created order as it bears the darkness of transformation.

While Sebastian Moore relies on Jungian psychology and Walter Wink uses social analysis, René Girard is a cultural anthropologist who comes to similar conclusions about evil and its reversal.[22] He begins

---

20 Wink, *Engaging the Powers,* 141.

21 For a careful argument about the ways in which God intended or caused Jesus's crucifixion, see Laughlin, *Jesus and the Cross,* chap. 2.

22 For a sampling of Girard's work, see René Girard, *Violence and the Sacred* (Baltimore: Johns Hopkins University Press, 1977); René Girard, Jean-Michel Oughourlian, and Guy Lefort, *Things Hidden since the Foundation of the World* (Stanford: Stanford University Press, 1987); René Girard, *I See Satan Fall Like Lightning,* trans. James G. Williams (Maryknoll, NY: Orbis Books, 2001). Walter Wink has an extended discussion of Girard and his scapegoat hypothesis in *Engaging the Powers,* 144–55.

by focusing on human desire and its consequences.[23] According to Girard, what drives social and cultural meaning and practice is *mimetic desire*—the yearning to imitate others whom we admire. We take on heroes or role models and act in accordance with their standards. But this desire for the good we admire in another leads ultimately to conflict; our loving of what they have or do becomes a coveting. We want to have what the model has or be what she is. Without some kind of safeguards or guidelines (which religion and culture usually provide), this desire can become a competition with the one we want to emulate. Alternatively, we compete with one another to replicate what we see as desirable in our heroes.

Either way, the operation of mimetic desire can lead to what Girard calls "scandal." This is when a person or group feels itself blocked from the object of power, prestige, or property that their idol possesses or is imagined to possess. When a number of these scandals exist, social tension can build up to the point where those involved must "let off steam" or the social milieu will fall apart. The easiest way to relieve this tension is for the group to find a victim upon which it can focus its frustration. This victim is blamed for the social tension and, in the extreme, killed in order to restore peace and harmony. This is what Girard calls the "single victim mechanism." He emphasizes that the development of tension due to mimetic desire and its release in finding and blaming a scapegoat is entirely unconscious. And he borrows biblical language to designate "Satan" as a name for the whole process of blaming and eradicating a scapegoat in order to resolve a community's problems. The real cause of social unrest is the contagion of mimetic desire run amuck (scandal). Satan is the mechanism by which someone who is weak, marginal, or different from the social norm is accused and punished in order to restore social order and mask the true problems at large.[24]

The role of myth in culture and religion, Girard contends, is to disguise the real violence involved here. Myths provide narrative justification for transferring blame to one who is innocent. They serve to cover

---

23 For a brief summary of Girard's thought, especially as it pertains to the biblical tradition, see James G. Williams, "Foreword," in Girard, *I See Satan*, ix–xxiii.

24 An example of this mechanism is the lynching of African-American slaves in the American south between the Civil War and World War II. This is documented in the report, *Lynching in America: Confronting the Legacy of Racial Terror* (Montgomery AL: Equal Justice Initiative, 2015). See www.eji.org.

up the wrongful violence involved and protect the unconsciousness of the actual problem. They serve the crowd, the majority, who bully and taunt the scapegoat in the belief that they are truly solving the problem of evil in their midst. Ironically, since destroying the scapegoat in the end produces harmony and restores peace in a community, that same victim becomes deified. In what Girard calls "double transference," after transferring blame onto the victim, the community transfers credit for the restoration of peace to the same victim. Since this person has been able to solve the community's problem, he or she must be a different sort of being—divine. Myths perpetuate both the initial victimization and its deification through covering over the truth of the initial conflict and the innocence (and humanity) of the victim.

Girard bases his framework on research into religion and culture, covering many millennia. However, this scapegoat phenomenon is readily observable—from the outside—in many contemporary contexts. From schoolyard bullying to family dynamics to the treatment of marginalized races or ethnic groups, we can see how a person or group takes on the characteristics of "the evil one" so that it/she/he can be destroyed, maintaining the status quo in a social group. Mostly, we see this in retrospect, historically, or by observing cultures other than our own. We often don't see it in ourselves or in our own circle since, by nature, it operates unconsciously.

At face value, it would seem that the story of Jesus's death fits neatly into this ongoing scapegoating cycle. Blame is laid on one who is proclaimed the disturber of the peace and his elimination restores balance—in this case both political and religious balance. However, Girard insists that the biblical record establishes the possibility of the end to mimetic violence precisely because it brings attention to the innocence of those who serve as scapegoats. He uses the story of Joseph in the Old Testament to illustrate this, and finds the key to the Christ story to be the sinlessness of the incarnate Word. To quote him:

> Before Christ and the Bible the satanic accusation was always victorious by virtue of the violent contagion that imprisoned human beings within systems of myth and ritual. The Crucifixion reduces mythology to powerlessness by exposing violent contagion, which is so effective in the myths that it prevents communities

from ever finding out the truth, namely, the innocence of their victims. . . . Jesus, in showing his innocence in the Passion accounts, has "cancelled" this accusation, he has "set it aside." He nails the accusation to the cross, which is to say that he reveals its falsity.[25]

Girard further attributes the overturning of this cycle of violence to the resurrection and the power of the Spirit in those who witnessed it:

> But on the third day of the Passion the scattered disciples re-group again about Jesus, who they believe is risen from the dead. Something happens in extremis that never happens in myths. A protesting minority appears and resolutely rises up against the unanimity of the persecuting crowd. . . . Where did they suddenly find the strength to oppose the crowd and the Jerusalem authorities? How do we explain this turnabout so contrary to all we have learned of the irresistible power of mimetic escalation?
>
> Until now I have always been able to find plausible responses to the questions posed in this book within a purely commonsensical and "anthropological" context. This time, however, *it is impossible.* To break the power of mimetic unanimity, we must postulate a power superior to violent contagion. . . .
>
> The Resurrection is not only a miracle, a prodigious transgression of natural laws. It is the spectacular sign of the entrance into the world of a power superior to violent contagion. . . .
>
> What is this power that triumphs over mimetic violence? The Gospels respond that it is the Spirit of God, the third person of the Trinity, the Holy Spirit. The Spirit takes charge of everything. It would be false, for example, to say the disciples "regained possession of themselves": it is the Spirit of God that possesses them and does not let them go.[26]

---

25 Girard, *I See Satan*, 138.
26 Ibid., 188–89.

What all of these approaches to the redemptive significance of Jesus's death and resurrection have in common is the law of the cross whereby God resolves the problem of sin and its consequences not by force or violence or coercion but through the transformation of minds and hearts via a complete reversal of common expectations; new life arises out of death and destruction. At the heart of this account are several key elements.[27] First, it negates a view of atonement as a logical deduction or a straightforward transaction. Indeed it is the *failure* to meet power with power, the *failure* of the logical, naturally expected transaction that opens up new *super*natural possibilities. Second, it involves the exposure of the ultimate unreality of evil through its manifestation against One who is fully human yet completely undeserving of retribution. The revelation of Jesus's innocence unveils what masks as justice to be merely an oppressive lust for power. Finally, Jesus's resurrection is as much a part of redemption as is his death. It is the empty tomb and the newly constituted body of the crucified one in the midst of the disciples that manifests what is truly real: divine love for humankind, even in its self-imposed enmity to God. And the reality of this divine love becomes instantiated through the presence of the Holy Spirit in a radically altered community—the Church. At the heart of all of it is a graced reversal of worldly expectations that yields new minds and hearts, persons forgiven and healed, living and seeing the world in an entirely altered way.

# Appropriating the Offer, Entering the Story

As we have maintained all along, these events and their meanings do not merely pertain to an era long ago. Nor is their significance a matter of claiming for ourselves some set of privileges won for us by a transaction in which Jesus suffered what we currently deserve. Rather, the transformation of evil and its consequences remains an opportunity for us today as much as for the first generation of believers. It comes to us through that generation of believers. Convinced that God had indeed done something radically new in the world, and that it had to do with the victory of

---

27 See conclusions in Crysdale, *Embracing Travail*, 155–56.

the divine good over evil and its consequences, they set out to proclaim the Good News to the world(s) that they inhabited. Furthermore, they were convinced that the same Spirit that raised Jesus from the dead was in their midst. So they not only preached, but invited the Spirit into their lives through participating in Jesus's death and resurrection in baptism and the repetition of the Lord's Supper. Generation after generation, the church discovered and rediscovered the joy of divine friendship, especially as such divine intimacy heals the brokenness of sin and alienation. The mediation of this friendship and reconciliation through the Spirit has taken place in myriad ways in myriad times and cultures; the church has had to learn anew with each mission and each generation just how the Good News is incarnated in its era.

The task of Christians today is to hear the gospel anew and to abide in its mysterious meaning. This is done through faithfulness in a community of faith, hearing the Scriptures as they are read and preached, participating in sacraments, and living lives of service. To receive God's meaning in all of this is to participate in a relationship, to abide in intimacy with the Triune God and to allow its concrete meaning for us to unfold.

There are two moments in the receiving of this communication, the revelation of God in "man's making of man." The first is to discover oneself in the narrative. Like any good drama, the Christian narrative is only effective if one is drawn into it, if one identifies with the characters and their struggles. Here let me emphasize what is not explicit in Moore or Wink or Girard. In the drama that exposes the cruelty and injustice that is at the heart of the crucifixion events, the hubris of the Powers as well as the betrayal of the disciples is in the foreground. Jesus on the cross represents the fruits of sin, whether it is of those who held power or of those who ran away frightened. The resurrection is about the forgiveness of sins. But for many, in that day and in ours, the choice to follow or pronounce judgment is not even an option. There are those on the "underside" of history who are the victims, over and over again; victims of poverty, of bigotry, of misogyny, of class discrimination. This victimization has become salient in the last two centuries as we have begun to realize that history is told by the dominant culture and leaves many behind or invisible.

So while there is a place for finding ourselves in Pilate or the Jewish authorities or Peter as they judge and betray Jesus, there is also a place for discovering ourselves as the one who is unjustly betrayed, humiliated, and killed. In addition to the myth of redemptive violence, there is the myth of redemptive suffering. And just as the death and resurrection overturns the one, so also it inverts the other. Just as the law of the cross reveals the futility of violence as the solution to sin, so it reveals that suffering does not in and of itself yield closeness to God. In both cases the grace of God needs to reverse the cycle of moral impotence and decline: by healing the broken and oppressed ones and forgiving the perpetrators and betrayers. In this process the decline of sin becomes a cycle of restoration: the forgiven are enabled to heal the wounded and the wounded are in turn empowered to forgive the perpetrators.[28]

The second moment in receiving God's communication is to choose to enter the narrative as it continues to unfold. Not only does one discover oneself in the story, one opts to contribute to its current manifestation. One moves from identifying with Jesus to following Jesus. One becomes an agent of redemption oneself. This choosing to follow will most likely mean embracing pain, choosing to love, forgiving others without recompense, seeking justice not revenge. So while suffering in itself does not yield reconciliation, the love behind and within reconciliation may yield suffering. Just as Jesus was about love that led to self-sacrifice, so our transformation in love will lead us to follow him to whatever cross we are called to in our lives.

A few corollaries here are warranted. First, it is important to stress that, just as suffering in itself does not directly yield salvation, so Jesus did not directly choose suffering as means of divine reconciliation.[29] What Jesus chose was love. In choosing love and its consequences in a hostile world, he simultaneously accepted suffering. Likewise, our choice to enter into Jesus's story may result in suffering, but what we

---

28 See Crysdale, *Embracing Travail*, chaps. 5 and 6.

29 In spite of misreadings of his work, Anselm nuances his own argument to make this same point. See our discussion in chapter three above.

choose is positive, to be in communion with the Risen Lord, the Fount of Life, and the Spirit, to love the world with their love.[30]

Second, the primary catalyst for reconciliation is not guilt as much as it is grief and sorrow arising from the discovery of love. As the sinless one, Jesus's experience of sin was that of other peoples' sins, not his own. As a divine friend of/with the other divine persons, his encounter with the brokenness of humanity yielded neither guilt for his own sins nor revenge for the injustice he suffered. Instead, his incarnate love was embodied in the great sorrow he felt for those broken ones who were alienated from themselves and God.[31] Likewise, as participants in the story, our primary mode of following is one of love, a love that grieves for both our own brokenness and that of others. Remorse for wrongdoing may be a stimulus for change, but true transformation comes as a result of being loved and such transformative love produces "good grief" as we mourn the harm we have done and the harm done to us. Just as revenge rarely creates justice, so preaching guilt seldom brings about graced transformation.

Finally, the two moments of discovering ourselves in the story and moving it forward are intimately connected. In order to fully understand oneself in the Jesus story, one needs to become an author of the story, to imitate Jesus, to undertake the resistance and surrender that will make one not only a recipient of salvation but an agent of salvation. Thus the opposition of "objective" and "subjective" atonement breaks down. Events that happened in history generate meanings that

---

30 This directly subverts what has been called the "cult of suffering" whereby suffering itself yields reconciliation/redemption. This presumption has over the centuries been applied inequitably to those who are not part of the dominant culture, such that greater suffering on the part of women, the "heathen" in Africa, the "barbarians" in South America, or other minorities has been rationalized due to their greater need for salvation. For one analysis of this phenomenon in regard to the missions in South America, see Yacob Tesfai, ed., *The Scandal of a Crucified World: Perspectives on the Cross and Suffering* (Maryknoll, NY: Orbis Books, 1994).

31 Lonergan says, "The sufferings of Christ, then, are the expression of God's detestation of sin. They are also the expression of Christ's own detestation of sin. . . . His detestation of sin, combined with his love of us, caused in him the greatest sorrow that we had sinned. He was sorry for our sins because of his love for us in a manner that we can hardly be sorry, because we do not possess his knowledge of God and his love of God. Christ, the Son of God, because of his perfect knowledge and love of his Father, could detest sin as sin is to be detested, and because of his love of us could feel a sorrow such as no sorrow can equal" (Lonergan, *Papers*, 22). The Anglican divine R. C. Moberly (1845–1903) presented Christ as the perfect penitent and focused on his sorrow for sin. See R. C. Moberly, *Atonement and Personality* (New York: Longmans, Green, and Co., 1901).

change lives, which in turn alters people, events, and meanings, creating new conditions of possibility for further transformation. What happened in the world changes us, who in turn change what happens in the world.

## Illustrations: Lives Transformed

Let us conclude this analysis with a few examples of people who discovered the power of divine friendship and chose to promote radical resurrection love in their situations. Some of these people have become well known for their stories while others are simply ordinary persons who discovered death, new life, and mission *in situ* as it were.

Martin Luther King Jr. (1929–1968) is well known for his role in the American civil rights movement. In 1963 a set of his sermons was published, entitled *Strength to Love*.[32] All of these were preached after the Montgomery bus boycott of 1955–1956. In one sermon he admits that he faced few challenges in his first twenty-four years of life. "I had no basic problems or burdens. Because of concerned and loving parents who provided for my every need, I sallied through high school, college, theological school, and graduate school without interruption. It was not until I became a part of the leadership of the Montgomery bus protest that I was actually confronted with the trials of life."[33]

Shortly after he became involved in this antisegregation work, he began to receive threatening phone calls. At first he assumed that they came from a marginal group and were of no concern. Eventually he realized that these opponents were in earnest and he began to be afraid. He continues the story:

> After a particularly strenuous day I settled into bed at a late hour. My wife had already fallen asleep and I was about to doze off when the telephone rang. An angry voice said, "Listen, nigger, we've taken all we want from you. Before next week you'll be sorry you ever came to Montgomery." I hung up, but could not sleep. It seemed

---

32 Martin Luther King Jr., *Strength to Love* (Cleveland: Collins Publishers, 1963).
33 Ibid., 112.

that all of my fears had come down on me all at once. I had reached the saturation point.

I got out of bed and began to walk the floor. Finally, I went to the kitchen and heated a pot of coffee. I was ready to give up. I tried to think of a way to move out of the picture without appearing to be a coward. In this state of exhaustion, when my courage had almost gone, I determined to take my problem to God. My head in my hands, I bowed over the kitchen table and prayed aloud. . . . "I am here taking a stand for what I believe is right. But now I am afraid. The people are looking to me for leadership, and if I stand before them without strength and courage, they too will falter. I am at the end of my powers. I have nothing left. I've come to the point where I can't face it alone."

At that moment I experienced the presence of the Divine as I had never before experienced him. It seemed as though I could hear the quiet assurance of an inner voice, saying, "Stand up for righteousness, stand up for truth. God will be at your side forever." Almost at once my fears began to pass from me. My uncertainty disappeared. I was ready to face anything. The outer situation remained the same, but God had given me an inner calm.

Three nights later, our home was bombed. Strangely enough, I accepted the word of the bombing calmly. My experience with God had given me a new strength and trust. I knew now that God is able to give us the interior resources to face the storms and problems of life. [34]

This excerpt comes from a sermon entitled "Our God Is Able." Here King confronts the seriousness of the evil he and his congregation are facing and yet proclaims with great confidence that God's power is great enough to rule the universe and reverse the evils of racism. As we now know, King's faith was still to confront some of the greatest challenges of his ministry, including dissension within his own ranks and further

---

[34] Ibid., 113–14.

violence from his enemies, culminating in his own assassination in 1968. His story illustrates the love of God transforming his life. It shows as well how this love led him to follow Jesus, even unto death.

A somewhat less dramatic story comes from a woman we will call Carolyn who exercises her ministry as a lay leader in The Episcopal Church. Carolyn grew up in the midwestern United States in a family that was isolated from its community and church by her mother's mental illness, an illness that was not well understood in the 1960s. Carolyn had no role models to follow and little guidance in social behavior. Nevertheless, she says, "I found a loving God. I came to see that on the cross Jesus lived into his belief in love so deeply that it transcended his own suffering and showed the most profound truth—that of divine love working in human life. I believed that path could transform my life."[35]

While Carolyn felt that she was a prisoner to the emotional abandonment she had experienced, she clung to her faith and was determined to learn more. She earned a Master of Divinity, learning more about God's love and working to live in a way that would draw her more deeply into redemption. In turn she was able to proclaim that path of redemption to others in both word and deed. Along the way she met and married Ben, who, at the conclusion of his theological education, was ordained to the priesthood. Carolyn saw her vocation unfolding as a layperson but hoped that she and Ben could cooperate and devise a shared ministry. Ben became rector of a large congregation in Ohio and the two built up the church together. Carolyn began many ministries, including planning creative liturgies and adult education programs. She hoped that when their children were older, she could take a paid position in the church that would deepen her ability to give testimony to "the way of the cross being the way of life."

In the meantime, Ben's own issues with his family of origin began colliding with congregational ministry. He became frightened and overwhelmed by his role in a system with large expectations. Carolyn fell into the crosshairs of these issues. Ben, despite being able to engage in meaningful conversations with her, was not able to collaborate in significant ways either at church or at home, nor to acknowledge Carolyn's own legitimate calling. She came to see that she needed to withdraw from her role in the congregation and she passed her leadership on to new

---

35 Private e-mail from author, April 10, 2015.

facilitators. As she withdrew, she once again found herself isolated and misunderstood. She felt that Ben had simply used her talents and presence without recognizing her call or message. A spiritual director that Carolyn consulted gave the alienation she felt from the congregation and her husband a name: she had been marginalized as a "scapegoat."

Well-intentioned church people admonished her simply to set aside her concerns and to be more supportive of her husband's ministry. Other friends and confidants advised her to leave a dysfunctional marriage in which she was not thriving. Nevertheless, Carolyn deeply loved Ben and he genuinely wanted to understand her position. They both realized that it was their personal psychic histories that were colliding. Carolyn clung to a belief in the redemptive power of the Spirit. She and Ben both chose to trust that redemption—in the form of renewed understanding, love, and commitment—would come to their situation.

So Carolyn stayed in the marriage. The two of them worked hard at learning how to listen to one another. Carolyn had to let go, over and over again, of her idealized image of working with Ben professionally and being part of his parish. Very gradually they came to discover the ways in which they could work together without the undermining patterns they were used to. They focused on bringing their work to fruition—including the raising of their three sons and Carolyn's new work with an international church agency.

There are still parts of their stories that are unresolved. At the same time there is a richness to their lives and ministries that is born out of their struggles. Their marriage is stronger and more satisfying than ever. They take upon themselves the task of seeking to understand the dynamics of scapegoating and of extending care to possible scapegoats. They have found ways of listening carefully to each other, of processing each other's challenges, of enjoying their extended families and sharing projects of hospitality and service.

Carolyn concludes her narrative with the following reflection. "As an adolescent trusting Jesus's path of suffering and redemption, I could not have imagined how demanding, how painful and difficult, this path would be for my particular life. But that early understanding has proven reliable. Redemption *has* come and *is* coming. Grace continues to win in new and surprising ways."[36]

---

36 Ibid.

As a final example, let us turn to the life of Dorothy Day (1897–1980). In the 1920s, Day was a radical communist living in New York City and committed to the plight of the poor. She lived and worked in a community of radical leftists and alienated intellectuals, all of whom believed that religion was the "opiate of the masses," merely a ploy by those in power to keep the marginalized from protesting. After a time she settled into a common law marriage with Foster Batterham. In 1926 she was thrilled to discover that she was pregnant. It was this pregnancy, along with Foster's love of nature, that brought her to a point of acknowledging the divine and falling in love with this beautiful creator God. She says of Foster, "I had known Foster a long time before we contracted our common-law relationship, and I have always felt that it was life with him that brought me natural happiness, that brought me to God."[37] Ironically, her new faith became a barrier between them: "His ardent love of creation brought me to the Creator of all things. But when I cried out to him, 'How can there be no God, when there are all these beautiful things,' he turned from me uneasily and complained that I was never satisfied."[38]

In due course, she and Foster separated. Day decided to have her daughter Teresa baptized and in the process she was convinced to become a Roman Catholic herself. She retained her radical views about social inequity and so was at home in neither the religious world nor the communist one. Her newfound church thought her politics odd and her old friends felt she had capitulated to the false consciousness promoted by religion. But she found continuity through love of both God and the crowds of ordinary yet pious believers:

> One of the disconcerting facts about the spiritual life is that God takes you at your word. Sooner or later one is given a chance to prove his love. The very word "diligo," the Latin word used for "love," means "I prefer." It was all very well to love God in His works, in the beauty of His creation which was crowned for me by the birth of my child. Forster had made the physical world come alive for me and had awakened in my heart a flood of gratitude. The final object of this love and gratitude was

---

37 Dorothy Day, *The Long Loneliness: The Autobiography of Dorothy Day* (San Francisco: Harper & Row, 1952), 134.

38 Ibid.

God. No human creature could receive or contain so vast a flood of love and joy as I often felt after the birth of my child. With this came the need to worship, to adore. I had heard many say that they wanted to worship God in their own way and did not need a Church in which to praise Him, nor a body of people with whom to associate themselves. But I did not agree to this. My very experience as a radical, my whole make-up, led me to want to associate myself with others, with the masses, in loving and praising God.[39]

Day did struggle with the wealth and privilege of the church and its minsters. She recognized the hypocrisy of an institution that preached radical love and social reform yet enjoyed the entitlements of social position. In 1933, along with Peter Maurin, she established the Catholic Worker Movement, involving a newspaper and a group of urban communities and farms dedicated to promoting the justice and the charity of Jesus.[40] She spent her days living in voluntary poverty, in love with the underclasses of ordinary folks. Late in life she was asked to write about how the social teaching of the Catholic Church had drawn her in. Her response was, "But I knew nothing of the social teaching of the Church at that time. I had never heard of the encyclicals. I felt that the Church was the Church of the poor, that St. Patrick's had been built from the pennies of servant girls, that it cared for the emigrant, it established hospitals, orphanages, day nurseries, houses of the Good Shepherd, homes for the aged, but at the same time, I felt that it did not set its face against a social order which made so much charity in the present sense of the word necessary."[41]

Day concludes her autobiography with the following prose poem:

We were just sitting there talking when Peter Maurin came in.

We were just sitting there talking when lines of people began to form, saying, "We need bread." We could not say, "Go, be thou filled." If there were six small loaves and a few fishes, we had to divide them. There was always bread.

39 Ibid., 139.
40 See http://www.catholicworker.org. Accessed June 9, 2015.
41 Day, *Long Loneliness*, 150.

We were just sitting there talking and people moved in on us. Let those who can take it, take it. Some moved out and that made room for more. And somehow the walls expanded.

We were just sitting there talking and someone said, "Let's all go live on a farm."

It was as casual as that, I often think. It just came about. It just happened.

I found myself, a barren woman, the joyful mother of children. It is not easy always to be joyful, to keep in mind the duty of delight.

The most significant thing about *The Catholic Worker*, is poverty, some say.

The most significant thing is community, others say. We are not alone any more.

But the final word is love. At times it has been, in the words of Father Zossima, a harsh and dreadful thing, and our very faith in love has been tried through fire.

We cannot love God unless we love each other, and to love we must know each other. We know Him in the breaking of bread, and we know each other in the breaking of bread, and we are not alone any more. Heaven is a banquet and life is a banquet, too, even with a crust, where there is companionship.

We have all known the long loneliness and we have learned that the only solution is love and that love comes with community.

It all happened while we sat there talking and it is still going on.[42]

# Conclusion

We have encountered a number of stories in which ordinary lives are changed in ways both large and small through an encounter with God. These encounters come spontaneously in the concrete worlds in which

---

42 Ibid., 285–86.

we live and work. Sometimes they are dramatic, sometimes they are simple movements of the heart, sometimes there are situations that call us to courageous choices. God meets us where we are. We can offer ourselves; we can attend to the deep longings of our hearts; we can undertake disciplines in order to grow closer to God. But the initial work of grace is utterly gratuitous and not under our control. Once touched, we have choices, about how to respond, about whether to live into the radically new horizons that are presented to us. The gift of grace comes repeatedly through life, and our choices about responding never cease.

These journeys are about relationships; relationships with others but most of all relationship with God. The heart of God's movement toward us and our response is love; deep intimate friendship within the deep love that is God the Trinity. These journeys are also about transformation—the transformation of repentance, sorrow, and forgiveness for our failings, and the transformation of healing and restoration from wounds suffered. The possibility of such transformation reached a particular climax in history twenty-one centuries ago with the advent of Jesus of Nazareth, a Jew by heritage and training but also the second person of the Trinity made human. His person, his teachings, his actions, and his death and resurrection communicated the love of God in continuity with the Jewish tradition yet revealed the possibility of a new order of life. His generation and those since encountered God in him and in the resurrection Spirit that continues in the church today.

Many images, metaphors, stories, and examples have been used to communicate the essence of this radical offer of a new way of being in the God-human connection. Redemption, atonement, sacrifice, adoption, justification, military triumph—all have served in this capacity. In time there was a move toward a more theoretical rendering of this reconciliation between God and man, with refinements of technical terms such as satisfaction. Our own cultural era has moved into a new realm of meaning—that of the turn to the subject, with its recognition of meaning-making and autonomous agency, of historical and cultural diversity, and of the "underside" of history whereby the dominant culture interprets the meaning of events, rendering others and their stories invisible. This later turn has revealed, in turn, the pervasive violence that seems to be inherent in religion itself. The Christian theology of atonement has come under special scrutiny since it appears to make a violent event—the crucifixion—the turning point in reconciling God and humans in their sinfulness. One person of the Trinity—the Son—suffers violent action by the will of another person of the Trinity—the Father—so that human persons will not suffer the same violent retribution.

In fact, as this book has sought to show, the heart of the Christian tradition of atonement is not about divine violence. While God, including the incarnate Son, abhors the evil that occurs in "man's making of man" and its systemic consequences, the divine response is love whereby detestation of sin becomes grief and sorrow over sin. Justice is restored not through vengeance but through self-sacrificial love. What occurs on the cross and through the cross is not a matter of power against power, nor an exercise of violent force. What occurs on the cross is the ironic reversal of power differentials. By allowing evil to express itself to its full extent—the unjust execution of the One who in no way deserved it—evil and its power mongering is exposed for what it is. Here is one violent action that in no way can be rationalized or justified; the self-serving motives behind it are revealed for all to see. The deeper justice-power-love of God is manifested in the resurrection and in the presence of the Spirit amongst believers in its aftermath.

So it continues today. Our failings are not restored through payment. Our alienation, from ourselves, our loved ones, our communities, is not overcome merely by balancing an account of some kind. Our suffering at the hands of others is not healed through retaliation. Instead we need an entirely new viewpoint, a renewed willingness to love and a revitalized openness to being loved. This comes only through gift— it is something we can seek but not anything we can achieve or create. Likewise, as agents of reconciliation, we too must embrace the challenge of self-sacrificing love. When a new horizon is granted us, we can become agents of salvation by forgiving others their sins and welcoming restorative love with all its painful challenges.

T. S. Elliot captures the ebb and flow of reception and action in our relationship with God. We can never fix what ails the world. We can only engage in a "lifetime's death in love" so that we can be present to the unattended moment, the hints and the guesses of ongoing Incarnation.

Men's curiosity searches past and future
And clings to that dimension. But to apprehend
The point of intersection of the timeless
With time, is an occupation for the saint—
No occupation either, but something given
And taken, in a lifetime's death in love,
Ardour and selflessness and self-surrender.
For most of us, there is only the unattended
Moment, the moment in and out of time,
The distraction fit, lost in a shaft of sunlight,
The wild thyme unseen, or the winter lightning
Or the waterfall, or music heard so deeply
That it is not heard at all, but you are the music
While the music lasts. These are only hints and guesses,
Hints followed by guesses; and the rest
Is prayer, observance, discipline, thought and action.
The hint half guessed, the gift half understood, is Incarnation.[43]

---

43 From "The Dry Salvages" in *Four Quartets,* http://www.paikassociates.com/pdf/ fourquartets.pdf, 19–20. See also http://www.coldbacon.com/poems/fq.html. Accessed June 12, 2015.

# Bibliography

## Introduction

Bailie, Gil. *Violence Unveiled: Humanity at the Crossroads*. New York: Crossroad, 1995.

Baker, Mark D., and Joel B. Green. *Recovering the Scandal of the Cross: Atonement in New Testament and Contemporary Contexts*. Downers Grove, IL: InterVarsity Press, 2011.

Brown, JoAnn Carlson, and Carole Bohn, eds. *Christianity, Patriarchy and Abuse: A Feminist Critique*. New York: Pilgrim Press, 1989.

Chadwick, Henry. *The Early Church*. London: Penguin Books, 1993.

Crysdale, Cynthia S. W. *Embracing Travail: Retrieving the Cross Today*. New York: Continuum, 1999.

Dawkins, Richard. *The God Delusion*. Boston: Houghton Mifflin Co., 2006.

Finlan, Stephen. *Options on Atonement in Christian Thought*. Collegeville, MN: Liturgical Press, 2007.

————. *Problems with Atonement*. Collegeville, MN: Liturgical Press, 2005.

Girard, René. *I See Satan Fall Like Lightning*. Translated by James G. Williams. Maryknoll, NY: Orbis Books, 2001.

Heim, S. Mark. *Saved from Sacrifice: A Theology of the Cross*. Grand Rapids, MI: William B. Eerdmans, 2006.

Hughes, Robert Davis. "What a Friend We Have in Jesus." *Sewanee Theological Review* 35 (1992): 247–63.

Jersak, Brad, and Michael Hardin. *Stricken by God?: Nonviolent*

*Identification and the Victory of Christ.* Grand Rapids, MI: William B. Eerdmans, 2007.

Keshgegian, Flora A. "The Scandal of the Cross: Revisiting Anselm and His Feminist Critics." *Anglican Theological Review* 82 (2000): 475–92.

Schwager, Raymund. *Banished from Eden: Original Sin and Evolutionary Theory in the Drama of Salvation.* Translated by James G. Williams. London: Gracewing, 2005.

————. *Jesus in the Drama of Salvation: Toward a Biblical Doctrine of Redemption.* Translated by James G. Williams and Paul Haddon. New York: Crossroad, 1999.

Stead, Michael R., ed. *Christ Died for Our Sins: Essays on the Atonement.* Canberra, Australia: Barton Books, 2013.

Tambasco, Anthony J. *A Theology of Atonement and Paul's Vision of Christianity.* Collegeville, MN: Liturgical Press, 1991.

Tesfai, Yacob. *The Scandal of a Crucified World: Perspectives on the Cross and Suffering.* New York: Orbis Books, 1994.

Weaver, J. Denny. *The Nonviolent Atonement.* 2nd ed. Grand Rapids, MI: William B. Eerdmans, 2011.

# Chapter One

Baum, Gregory. *Religion and Alienation: A Theological Reading of Sociology.* New York: Paulist Press, 1975.

Dent, Barbara. *My Only Friend Is Darkness: Living the Night of Faith with St. John of the Cross.* Washington, DC: ICS Publications, 1992.

Fitzgerald, Constance. "Impasse and Dark Night." In *Women's Spirituality: Resources for Christian Development,* 2nd ed., edited by Joanne Wolski Conn, 410–35. New York, Paulist Press, 1996

Fowler, James W. *Becoming Adult, Becoming Christian: Adult Development and Christian Faith.* San Francisco: Harper & Row, 1984.

————. *Stages of Faith: The Psychology of Human Development and the Quest for Meaning.* San Francisco: Harper & Row, 1981.

Lonergan, Bernard J. F. "Dialectic of Authority." In *A Third Collection,* edited by Frederick E. Crowe, 5–12. New York: Paulist Press, 1985.

————. *Method in Theology.* New York: Seabury Press, 1972.

May, Gerald. *The Dark Night of the Soul: A Psychiatrist Explores the*

*Connection between Darkness and Spiritual Growth.* San Francisco: Harper San Fransciso, 2005.

Moore, Sebastian. *The Contagion of Jesus: Doing Theology As If It Mattered.* Maryknoll, NY: Orbis Books, 2007.

————. *Jesus: Liberator of Desire.* New York: Crossroad, 1989.

# Chapter Two

Baker, Mark D., and Joel B. Green. *Recovering the Scandal of the Cross: Atonement in New Testament and Contemporary Contexts.* Downers Grove, IL: InterVarsity Press, 2011.

Brown, Raymond E. *The Death of the Messiah: From Gethsemane to the Grave.* Vol. 1. New York: Doubleday, 1994.

————. "The Pater Noster as an Eschatological Prayer." In *New Testament Essays*, 275–320. New York: Image, 1968.

Bryan, Christopher. *A Preface to Romans.* New York: Oxford University Press, 2000.

————. *The Resurrection of the Messiah.* Oxford: Oxford University Press, 2011.

Cranfield, C. E. B. *The Epistle to the Romans.* 2 vols. The International Critical Commentary. Edinburgh: T & T Clark, 1975–79.

Dunn, James D. G. *Jesus Remembered.* Grand Rapids, MI: Eerdmans, 2003.

Finlan, Stephen. *Options on Atonement in Christian Thought.* Collegeville, MN: Liturgical Press, 2007.

————. *Problems with Atonement.* Collegeville, MN: Liturgical Press, 2005.

Fitzmyer, Joseph A. *Romans: A New Translation and Commentary.* The Anchor Bible. Vol. 33. New York: Doubleday, 1993.

Fredriksen, Paula. *Jesus of Nazarerth, King of the Jews: A Jewish Life and the Emergence of Christianity.* London: Macmillan, 1999.

Gambie, Harry. *The New Testament Canon: Its Making and Meaning.* Minneapolis: Fortress Press, 1985.

Jeremias, Joachim. *The Prayers of Jesus.* London: SCM, 1967.

Laughlin, Peter. *Jesus and the Cross: Necesity, Meaning, and Atonement.* Princeton Theological Monograph Series. Eugene, OR: Pickwick Publishers, 2014.

Levensen, Jon D. *Resurrection and the Restoration of Israel: The Ultimate Victory of the God of Life*. New Haven, CT: Yale University Press, 2006.

McKnight, Scot. *Jesus and His Death: Historiography, the Historical Jesus, and Atonement Theory*. Waco, TX: Baylor University Press, 2005.

Meier, John P. *A Marginal Jew: Rethinking the Historical Jesus*. Vol. 1. New York: Doubleday, 1991.

Metzger, Bruce. *The Canon of the New Testament: Its Origin, Development, and Significance*. New York: Oxford University Press, 1987.

Meyer, Ben F. *The Aims of Jesus*. London: SCM Press, 1979.

Sanders, E. P. *Paul: A Very Short Introduction*. Oxford: Oxford University Press, 1991.

Sloyan, Gerard S. *The Crucifixion of Jesus: History, Myth, Faith*. Minneapolis: Fortress Press, 1995.

Tambasco, Anthony J. *A Theology of Atonement and Paul's Vision of Christianity*. Collegeville, MN: Liturgical Press, 1991.

Wright, N. T. *Jesus and the Victory of God*. Minneapolis: Fortress Press, 1996.

———. *The New Testament and the People of God*. Minneapolis: Fortress Press, 1992.

# Chapter Three

Anselm of Canterbury. *Anselm of Canterbury: The Major Works*. Oxford World Classics. Oxford: Oxford University Press, 1998.

Augustine. *The Trinity*. Edited by John E. Rotelle. Translated by Edmund Hill. In *The Works of Saint Augustine: A Translation for the 21st Century*, part I, vol. 5. New York: New York City Press, 1991.

Aulen, Gustaf. *Christus Victor: An Historical Study of the Three Main Types of the Idea of Atonement*. Translated by A. G. Hebert. New York: MacMillan, 1969.

Baker, Mark D., and Joel B. Green. *Recovering the Scandal of the Cross: Atonement in New Testament and Contemporary Contexts*. 2nd ed. Downers Grove, IL: InterVarsity Press, 2011.

Baker, Denise N. *The Showings of Julian of Norwich*. New York: W. W. Norton, 2004.

Bernard of Clairvaux. *Bernard of Clairvaux: Selected Works*. Translated by Gillian R. Evans. New York: Paulist Press, 1987.

Dreyer, Elizabeth, ed. *The Cross in Christian Tradition: From Paul to Bonaventure*. New York: Paulist Press, 2000.

Finlan, Stephen. *Options on Atonement in Christian Thought*. Collegeville, MN: Liturgical Press, 2007.

Hefling, Charles. "A Perhaps Permanently Valid Achievement: Lonergan and Christ's Satisfaction." *Method: Journal of Lonergan Studies* 10 (1992): 51–76.

Loewe, William P. *Lex Crucis: Soteriology and the Stages of Meaning*. Minneapolis: Fortress Press, 2016.

Ray, Darby Kathleen. *Deceiving the Devil: Atonement, Abuse, and Ransom*. Cleveland: Pilgrim Press, 1998.

Sloyan, Gerard S. *The Crucifixion of Jesus: History, Myth, Faith*. Minneapolis: Fortress Press, 1995.

Weaver, J. Denny. *The Nonviolent Atonement*. 2nd ed. Grand Rapids, MI: Eerdmans, 2011.

# Chapter Four

Brondos, David A. *Fortress Introduction to Salvation and the Cross*. Minneapolis: Fortress Press, 2007.

Buckley, Michael J. *At the Origins of Modern Atheism*. New Haven, CT: Yale University Press, 1987.

Burns, Patout. "The Concept of Satisfaction in Medieval Redemption Theory." *Theological Studies* 36 (1975): 285–304.

Butterfield, Herbert. *The Origins of Modern Science, 1300–1800*. 2nd ed. New York: Free Press, 1966.

Crysdale, Cynthia, and Neil Ormerod. *Creator God, Evolving World*. Minneapolis: Fortress Press, 2013.

Darwin, Charles. *On the Origin of Species by Means of Natural Selection or the Preservation of Favoured Races in the Struggle for Life*. Mineola, NY: Dover., 2006.

Grensted, L. W. *A Short History of the Doctrine of the Atonement*. London: Longmans, Green and Co., 1920.

Hazard, Paul. *The European Mind: 1680–1715*. London: Hollis and Carter, 1953.

Kant, Immanuel. *Foundations of the Metaphysics of Morals* and *What Is Enlightenment?* Translated by L. W. Beck. New York: Liberal Arts Press, 1959.

Loewe, William P. *Lex Crucis: Soteriology and the Stages of Meaning.* Minneapolis: Fortress Press, 2016.

Lonergan, Bernard J. F. "Theology in Its New Context." In *Second Collection,* edited by William F. J. Ryan and Bernard J. Tyrrell, 55–68. London: Darton, Longman, and Todd, 1974.

Schweitzer, Albert. *The Quest of the Historical Jesus.* Edited by John Bowden. Minneapolis: Fortress Press, 2001.

Snobelen, Stephen. "Isaac Newton, Heretic: The Strategies of a Nicodemite." *British Journal for the History of Science* 32 (1999): 381–419.

Sobel, David. *Galileo's Daughter: A Historical Memoir of Science, Faith, and Love.* New York: Penguin Books, 2000.

Tyrrell, George. *Christianty at the Crossroads.* London: Longmans, Green and Co., 1909.

# Chapter Five

Augustine. *The Trinity.* In *The Works of Saint Augustine: A Translation for the 21st Century,* edited by John E. Rotelle, translated by Edmund Hill, part I, vol. 5. New York: New York City Press, 1991.

Crysdale, Cynthia S. W. "Expanding Lonergan's Legacy: Belief, Discovery and Gender." In *Christian Identity in a Postmodern Age*, edited by Declan Marmion, 65–90. Dublin: Veritas, 2005.

———. "Heritage and Discovery: A Framework for Moral Theology." *Theological Studies* 63 (2002): 559–78.

———. "Women and the Social Construction of Self-Appropriation." In *Lonergan and Feminism*, edited by Cynthia Crysdale, 88–113. Toronto: University of Toronto Press, 1994.

Doran, Robert M. *Theology and the Dialectics of History.* Toronto: University of Toronto Press, 1990.

Lonergan, Bernard. *Method in Theology.* New York: Seabury Press, 1972.

———. *Philosophical and Theological Papers, 1958–1964.* Vol. 6, Collected Works of Bernard Lonergan. Edited by Crowe Frederick E., Robert M. Doran, and Robert C. Croken. Toronto: University of Toronto Press, 1996.

———. "Theology in Its New Context." In *Second Collection*, edited by William F. J. Ryan and Bernard J. Tyrrell, 55–68. London: Darton, Longman, and Todd, 1974.

Taylor, Charles. *Sources of the Self: The Making of the Modern Identity.* Cambridge, MA: Harvard University Press, 1989.

# Chapter Six

Alsford, Sally. "Sin and Atonement in Feminist Perspective." In *Atonement Today*, edited by John Goldingay, 148–65. London: SPCK, 1995.

Aristotle. *The Nichomachean Ethics.* London: Penguin, 1976.

Crysdale, Cynthia S. W. *Embracing Travail: Retrieving the Cross Today.* New York: Continuum, 1999.

Day, Dorothy. *The Long Loneliness: The Autobiography of Dorothy Day.* San Francisco: Harper & Row, 1952.

Girard, René. *I See Satan Fall Like Lightning.* Translated by James G. Williams. Maryknoll, NY: Orbis Books, 2001.

———. *Violence and the Sacred.* Baltimore: Johns Hopkins University Press, 1977.

Girard, René, Jean-Michel Oughourlian, and Guy Lefort. *Things Hidden since the Foundation of the World.* Stanford, CA: Stanford University Press, 1987.

Goldstein, Valerie Saiving. "The Human Situation: A Feminine View." *Journal of Religion* 40 (1960): 100–112.

Hefling, Charles. "Lonergan's *Cur Deus Homo*: Revisiting the 'Law of the Cross.'" In *Meaning and History in Systematic Theology: Essays in Honor of Robert Doran, SJ*, edited by J. D. Dadosky, 145–66. Milwaukee: Marquette University Press, 2009.

King Jr., Martin Luther. *Strength to Love.* Cleveland: Collins Publishers, 1963.

Laughlin, Peter. *Jesus and the Cross: Necessity, Meaning, and Atonement.* Eugene, OR: Pickwick Publishers, 2014.

Lonergan, Bernard J. F. "Dialectic of Authority." In *A Third Collection*, edited by Frederick E. Crowe. New York: Paulist Press, 1985.

———. *Insight: A Study of Human Understanding.* Vol. 3, Collected Works of Bernard Lonergan. Edited by Crowe Frederick E. and Robert M. Doran. Toronto: University of Toronto Press, 1992.

———. *Philosophical and Theological Papers, 1958–1964*. Vol. 6, Collected Works of Bernard Lonergan. Edited by Frederick E. Crowe, Robert M. Doran, and Robert C. Croken. Toronto: University of Toronto Press, 1996.

———. *The Redemption*. Vol. 9, Collected Works of Bernard Lonergan. Edited by Robert M. Doran, Daniel Monsour, and Jeremy Wilkins. Translated by Michael Shields. Toronto: University of Toronto Press, forthcoming.

Moberly, R. C. *Atonement and Personality*. New York: Longmans, Green, and Co., 1901.

Moore, Sebastian. *The Crucified Is No Stranger*. London: Darton, Longman and Todd, 1977.

Plaskow, Judith. *Sex, Sin, and Grace*. Lanham, MD: University Press of America, 1980.

Tesfai, Yacob, ed. *The Scandal of a Crucified World: Perspectives on the Cross and Suffering*. Maryknoll, NY: Orbis Books, 1994.

Williams, Rowan. "The Body's Grace." In *Our Selves, Our Souls and Bodies*, edited by Charles Hefling, 58–68. Boston: Cowley Publications, 1996.

Wink, Walter. *Engaging the Powers: Discernment and Resistance in a World of Domination*. Minneapolis: Fortress Press, 1992.

# Index